The $15,000 Year

THE $15,000 YEAR

The iLifer's Guide to Riding Out the Recession

...and Changing the World.

Toluse Olorunnipa

73rd & Ps. Publishing Co.
Stanford, California
2009

Published by 73rd & Ps. Publishing Co.

73rd & Ps. Publishing Co.
895 Campus Drive, 133D
Stanford, CA 94309

PUBLISHER'S NOTE
This publication is designed to provide accurate and useful information in regard to the subject matter covered. It is sold with the understanding that the publisher is not engaged in rendering legal, accounting or other professional services. If you require such assistance, you should seek the services and advice of a trained professional.

LIBRARY OF CONGRESS CATALOGING-IN-PUBLICATION DATA
Olorunnipa, Toluse
The $15,000 year: the iLifer's guide to riding out the recession (and changing the world) / Toluse Olorunnipa.
p. cm.
Includes bibliographical references.
ISBN-13: 978-0-9823665-0-9
ISBN-10: 0-9823665-0-7
1. Finance, Personal—United States. 2. Young adults—Finance, Personal.
I. Title: The $15,000 Year. II. Title.

2009901997

First printing, 2009
Printed in the United States of America

XX123.Z45 2009

Book Design by Toluse Olorunnipa / 73rd & Ps. Publishing Co.

10 9 8 7 6 5 4 3 2 1

CONTENTS

PREFACE: A Message to the '09 Graduate

In the last few weeks you've probably spent time reminiscing about one of the most memorable and exciting periods of your life. You probably kicked it at all your favorite places, lounging on the quad with your old roommate, hanging out in the dorm with lifelong friends you will cherish forever as well as acquaintances whom you will only remain connected to through Facebook status updates. You may have spent some time looking back on the scrawny excuse for a young man or woman you were freshman year and thinking about all the challenges, term papers, failures, successes and drama-filled situations that have crafted you into the proud diploma-bearing graduate you are today. First and foremost, let me start by saying, Congrats.

Now, welcome to the Real World. The economy is in shambles, the job market is a shell of its former self and the apron strings have been cut. Pretty soon, you will be responsible for bills you didn't even know existed, required to make career choices more difficult than any midterm you ever crammed for and presented with financial decisions that will ultimately determine your future standard of living.

But, not to worry. This book is designed to get you through this pivotal period of transition and make sure you come out on the other side financially (and emotionally) sound.

If you received *The $15,000 Year* as a graduation gift from your school, a commencement speaker, a family member or a friend, this financial and personal guidebook couldn't be more appropriate given the senior year you had.

Think about it:

The running story of your graduation year has been the troubled economy: job losses, global recession, home foreclosures, 401(k) wipeouts and the like. The first month of massive job cuts (September 2008) took place at the beginning of your final fall semester and, for the rest of the school year, somewhere between 400,000 and 700,000 Americans lost their jobs every month.

Naturally, as the job market shed more than 5 million posts, those of you who were applying for your first full-time gig ran head on into one of the iciest recruiting seasons in recent history. Recruiters were particularly shy this year, as the number of job openings decreased to its lowest level since 2000 and those employers who did show up on college campuses said they expected to hire 22 percent fewer graduates from the class of 2009 than from the class of 2008. No industry was immune and, as retirement savings were obliterated by the stock market crash, college seniors found themselves competing against citizen seniors for work.

Given this reality, you may have found yourself Wikipediaing the "Dow Jones Industrial Average" to find out exactly what it is and why it was nose-diving. You probably paid closer attention to the business section of NYTimes.com or you may have visited a personal finance website for the first time. You may have accepted a position far outside of the lines of your ideal career path or resigned yourself to moving back in with your parents until you could find a suitable job.

Your conversations with your friends probably focused more on the challenges of the tough job market and less on who would win the rivalry game or which couple became Facebook official. Or, maybe you casually dismissed the economic bear in the room by repeating half-jokes like "Lucky us, why'd we have to graduate in the middle of a friggin Great Recession?" or, "I want to punch the economy in the face right now," or "Eff this, I'm definitely going straight to grad school now."

Maybe you're going straight to grad school now.

This book is written with a sensitivity to all of these scenarios and the advice you'll find in the pages ahead is designed to help you chart your way through this period of personal and economic uncertainty as smoothly as possible. The purpose of *The $15,000 Year* is to guide you through the rocky first year in the "Real World" and help you make a lot of the tough financial, occupational and lifestyle decisions that you'll face in the next few months. If you follow the guidelines of this book, you'll be able to save as much as $15,000 this year and use this cash to start an emergency fund, pay down those credit cards and student loans, invest in an entrepreneurial project, take a less lucrative job that allows you to give back and/or start putting money away for retirement.

But relax. This isn't one of those "frugal living" guides. I'm not trying to spoil your fun or make you live like an old penny-pincher. I realize (better than most) that your carefree 20s are the only years in your life when you can throw caution (and your credit) to the wind. This is the time when spontaneity can drive your decision-making (and your spending); when you're not responsible for taking care of anyone but yourself; when you can stay out until 2 a.m. on a Thursday night because Friday is, in fact, part of the weekend.

This is true, but, as you'll see in the pages ahead, you don't have to be financially reckless or aloof to live the good life. And, at the same time, you don't have to be a tightwad or a Wall Street type to save money and efficiently manage your finances. In fact, It's never been easier, more appropriate, or more "in" to save cash and this book will give you a road map for exactly how to do that. Thanks to the democratization of the 21st century marketplace and the money-saving power of technology, you can save $15,000 this year without living like a hippie or a miser.

Trust me, you won't find anything in the pages ahead about cloth diapers, dumpster diving, price books or mortgage refinancing. But you will learn how to save $1,100 on groceries by loading digital coupons onto your loyalty card or iPhone, how to rent and furnish your first apartment on the cheap, how to pay down those high-interest credit cards in months (not years) and how to start investing for your future now, when the payoffs are higher than they'll ever be.

I've scoured dozens of personal finance books and hundreds of frugal living websites and handpicked those tips that are appropriate for young, independent 20-somethings on the go. I've added a good deal of lesser-known strategies from my personal experiences as an undercover-cheapskate-turned-entrepreneur and *The $15,000 Year* is the result.

I hope you'll take advantage of this independent life stage, take the $15,000 Year challenge and make a few minor changes that will have you on the road to achieving financial stability and positive social impact in no time.

Your future You will thank you.

Definition: iLifer

1. Someone who is currently in the "Independent Life Stage," the period between childhood and childbearing. Due to a sharp rise in average age at first marriage, this life stage now lasts longer than ever. The average iLifer spends about 10 years living "independently" before getting married and having children—twice as long as the average young adult in 1975.

2. A person who grew up during the dawning of the Information Age. iLifers, also known as "Digital Natives," have never known a world without the Internet.

3. Anyone who revels in the liberty of being young, independent and relatively obligation-free in the 21st century. iLifers tend to exude positivity, optimism and spontaneity.

4. An indirect reference to "I" Lifers. These 20-somethings show high levels of self-esteem, self-focus and self-confidence during this life stage.

   Note: iLifers demonstrate high rates of civic engagement, espousing causes such as environmentalism and social equality. As the first generation of "global citizens," iLifers' worldview is particularly globally oriented.

   Synonyms: Millennials, Gen- Yers, Echo Boomers, Twixters.

PROLOGUE

iLifers. Defined.

Known by a long list of nicknames (including "Millennials" and "Gen-Yers"), iLifers were born in and around the 1980s and currently range in age from the mid-teens to the late 20s. Demographically and socially, today's young adults look almost nothing like previous generations of 20-somethings. They are waiting longer to get married, pioneering the digital revolution and fundamentally transforming the traditional models of civic engagement, occupational mobility and social communication.

They show a high affinity for changing the world and, if possible, would like to do so before they turn 30.

Before we jump into the "riding out the recession" part, let's take a look at a few of the distinct qualities of this cohort and find out exactly why these romantic young idealists might actually be on to something.

I. iLifers and the Independent Life Stage

The term "Independent Life Stage" (ILS) was coined by Stanford University professor Michael Rosenfeld in his 2007 book *The Age of Independence*. The book chronicles a major demographic shift that has occurred in recent American history, significantly affecting the life trajectories of today's young adults. This shift is driven by two main phenomena that have developed recently: the rise in median age at first marriage and the delaying of parenthood until the late twenties and early thirties. These trends, combined with higher rates of college enrollment, have led to the lengthening of the "independent" stage of life—the time when a young adult has left his or her parents' home but has not yet started his or her own family.

GRAPH 1: PERCENTAGE OF YOUNG UNMARRIED MEN AND WOMEN WHO HEAD THEIR OWN HOUSEHOLD 1880–2005

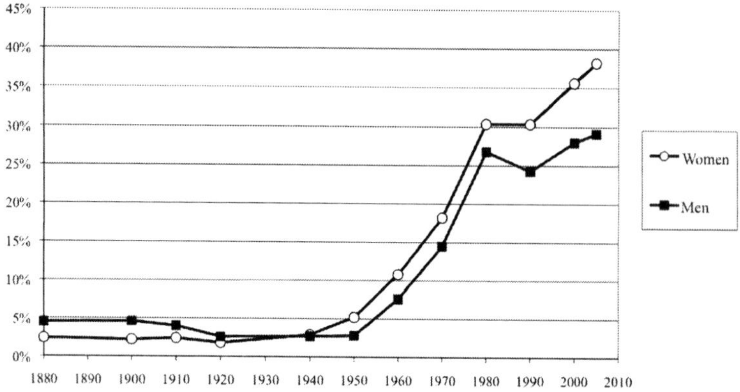

Source: weighted census microdata from 1880, 1900–1920, 1940–2000 via IPUMS, 2005 data from American Community Survey. Individuals are U.S. born, age 20–29, never married.

Such a period of youthful independence was basically nonexistent up until about 1960—but it has lengthened considerably during the last half-century and now lasts longer than ever. The traditional custom of adolescents living with their parents until they were ready to wed was first rejected by Baby Boomers in the 1960s as they pursued higher education in larger (and more gender-representative) numbers, nudged upwards the average age at first marriage and engaged in more countercultural activities (most of which were not conducive to child raising).

Young people today have picked up on that trend, transforming the time of independence from a short transitional period to into a full-scale life stage lasting close to a decade or longer. According to census figures, the median age at first marriage has risen by about five years since the 1960s (See Table 1). The median age for first-time brides increased from 20.8 in 1965 to 25.6 in 2008* and today the average man says "I do" at the age of 27-and-a-half (compared to 22.8 in 1965). These numbers are even higher for those for those who pursue advanced degrees.

> *"As recently as 1970, the typical 21-year-old was married or about to be married, caring for a newborn child or expecting one soon, done with education or about to be done and settled into a long-term job or the role of full-time mother.... Today, the life of a typical 21-year-old could hardly be more different. Marriage is at least five years off, often more. Ditto parenthood. Education may last several more years, through an extended undergraduate program—'the four year degree' in five, six, or more—and perhaps graduate or professional school."*
> —JEFFREY JENSEN ARNETT, *Emerging Adulthood* (2004)

The transformation of the Independent Life Stage is a significant phenomenon not simply because today's altars and delivery rooms are more mature than they've been in the past, but because young people are spending this decade of independence doing unique and dynamic things that will undoubtedly shape the future of America and the world in ways yet unknown. For example:

TABLE 1: Median Age at First Marriage (1950–2008)

YEAR	MALES	FEMALES
1950	22.8	20.3
1960	22.8	20.3
1970	23.2	20.8
1980	24.7	22.0
1990	26.1	23.9
1995	26.9	24.5
2000	26.8	25.1
2005	27.1	25.3
2008	27.5	25.6

Source: U.S. Census Bureau, Current Population Survey (2008)

We† change jobs every 18 months. We take a year to pursue theater in Manhattan or social justice in the Third World. Then we go to grad school. We volunteer our time and skills in ways that are distinctly 21st century: teaching for America, microlending, and Facebooking for a cause. The country's most diverse cohort, we spend time interacting with people from a wide range of backgrounds on our campuses, online and in the metropolitan cities we migrate to. We form distinct political views and rebel against the conventional concept of youth apathy.

And we distinguish ourselves from previous generations in a host of other ways—some of which will be highlighted in the next few pages.

*According to the National Center for Health Statistics, the average age of first-time mothers was 25.2 in 2005, a record high number, up from 21.4 in 1970).

†Since I'm currently a 1980s-born iLifer, I'll use "we" (instead of "they") throughout the rest of the book.

II. iLifers as "Digital Natives"

Unquestionably, the dominant phenomenon that has shaped the lives and outlooks of iLifers has been the dawning and rapid development of the digital era. The Information Age has been hailed as the most innovative and fast-moving period of technological transformation in history and its impact on those who came of age in the 1990s is unmistakable.

In *Born Digital,* tech experts John Palfrey and Urs Gasser refer to iLifers as the first generation of "Digital Natives," or those who were born and raised in the digital world. Comparing these tech-natives with "digital immigrants," or those born before the digital age, they find major differences in areas such as creative expression, self-efficacy and information processing.

As a result of our tech-heavy introduction to the world and its information, we spend more time online than any other age group and are the most active video uploaders, personal profile managers and information searchers on the Web. Because we've never really known a world without the Internet, we interact more naturally with digital devices (and sometimes have trouble performing seemingly simple tasks without them).

We are infatuated with innovation and are constantly attempting to be the visionaries behind the next hot invention, website or viral phenomenon. We drop out of college, move across the country and create the world's largest social networking website. (With our roommates.) We do much of our business online and are transforming the culture of the traditional marketplace. We share files, ignore ads and publish consumer reviews, alerting the digital world to the virtues and flaws of the latest products.

We're not quite sure how our parents and professors survived without cell phones, iPods, DVD players, navigation systems, the Internet and a host of other indispensable gadgets and services but we thank God for not bringing us into the world before digitizing it.

III. Livin' the iLife

The third definition focuses on the general temperament of iLifers during this lengthened period of freedom. With no live-in parents to scrutinize and reprimand our countercultural actions and no children or aging relatives to look after, we are in many ways the "freest" we will ever be.

And we know it.

In the period between departing from our parental nests and hatching our own eggs, we are (*sorry...*) free as a bird. We forge deeper connections with our friends and use technology to maintain our expansive social networks. We travel the country and the world, sleeping on couches, in hostels and in resorts.

We try new things and fail. We get up, try again, repeat, and eventually find something we're good at. We stay up chatting or partying with friends until 3 a.m., then drink a Red Bull and speed-write that report due the next morning. We tend to embrace an upbeat optimism, believing that things will work out and that we will be successful and happy in life*.

While it is certainly true that Boomers and Gen-Xers partied, traveled and tried all kinds of new things in their youths, the sheer length of time iLifers spend in this "young and free" life stage signals an important break from the past. For the first time in America's history, young adults are not only reveling in the liberating independence of youth, but also choosing to extend the party a little longer. Twenty-first century 20-somethings are opting to spend an increasing portion of their lives as single, independent ladies and gentlemen with an undivided obligation to self and self-development. This brings us to the final definition of iLifer.

IV. All About "I" Lifers *(A Time of Temporary Self-Focus)*

> *"You are special."*
>
> —FRED ROGERS of *Mister Rogers Neighborhood* (circa 1991)

Another social trend distinct to this generation is an increase in reported levels of self-focus, self-worth, self-efficacy and self-esteem. Generational scholars attribute this trend to a fusion of developments that have combined to make today's young adults feel special from birth through bachelor's degree.

Jean Twenge, author of *Generation Me*, points out that "reliable birth control, legalized abortion, and a cultural shift toward parenthood as a choice made us the most *wanted* generation of children in American history" (2006). Supporting this claim, federal data show that, between 1988 and 1999 (iLifers' prime childhood years), rates of substantiated

*According to a recent survey, 96 percent of 18- to 24-year-olds agree with the statement "I am very sure that someday I will get to where I want to be in life."

child abuse fell by 43 percent and missing children cases decreased by 51 percent.

As the first wave of iLifers entered elementary school in the late 1980s, the nation was championing a national school reform movement. Throughout the 1990s, the ideologies of the "self-esteem" movement merged with our traditional curricula and we were frequently reminded of our specialness between the hours of 8 a.m. and 3 p.m. In late afternoon Little League and gymnastics, we all received trophies regardless of our performance—with parent-coaches constantly reminding us that we were all winners.

As many of us entered junior high school in the mid- and late 1990s, our wellbeing came to dominate the national agenda. In *Millennials and the Pop Culture*, generational historians William Strauss and Neil Howe note that "by 1998, more than half of all Americans (a record share) said that 'getting kids off to the right start' ought to be the nation's top priority*" (2006).

From the heavily covered high school class of 2000 to the perpetually rehabbed starlets that now grace our magazines and even our cable news programs, the amount of media coverage, social scientific analysis, and literature that has been dedicated to analyzing and understanding iLifers has certainly been unprecedented.

There is conflicting evidence about whether all this attention has turned iLifers into narcissistic egoists, simply made us more self-confident and self-assured, or has had no lasting effect. On the one hand, iLifers tend to score relatively high marks on the Narcissistic Personality Index (NPI), a rubric for determining levels of self-absorption in individuals. On the other hand, social statistics have consistently shown that today's young adults demonstrate record high rates volunteerism and are actively involved in movements that address social ills both locally and globally.

Clark University professor Jeffrey Jensen Arnett offers what seems to be the most appropriate happy medium as a solution to this debate. In his 2004 book, *Emerging Adulthood*, he claims that 20-somethings, positioned at the determinative life stage between adolescence and adulthood, develop a *temporary* condition of self-focus, not a perma-

*For comparison, less than one in 10 Americans believed childhood education should be the nation's top priority in 2008.

nent disposition. In other words, we take this time to develop ourselves personally so that we can be prepared to be effective change agents once we do settle down, start our own families, and infiltrate the decision-making halls of politics, business, social service, law, science, media and entertainment. We take a few years to "find ourselves," sampling different jobs and cities so that we can discover which of these fields we are actually interested in pursuing.

While iLifers demonstrate relatively high levels of civic engagement and most of us list "helping others" as one of the main things we want to accomplish in our lives, the ILS is a once-in-a-lifetime period when we are our sole obligation. As a result, the evidence of our temporary narcissism and the extent to which we value our own ideas and input is quite clear:

We promote ourselves on YouTube and list our own utterances under the "Favorite Quotes" section of our Facebook pages. We "tweet," posting moment-by-moment updates on the progress of our daily errands online. In 2009, 5 million of us wrote "25 Random Things About Me" notes on Facebook in the span of about a week, publishing itemized declarations of our individuality for our close friends and the entire digital world. We speak up at work, offering ideas for revamping "outdated" business models and management structures, even if we've only been around for a few months. Armed with a fundamental belief in Mister Rogers' neighborly words of wisdom (he once said "each of us has something that no one else has, something inside that is unique to all time"), we take to the blogosphere and the startup circuit in record numbers, championing new forms of expression and challenging age-old market principles.

iLIFERS: IN A NUTSHELL

To review, today's 20-somethings are tech-savvy, not eager to rush into marriage or parenthood, somewhat self-focused (at least temporarily) and thoroughly enjoying a prolonged period of independent life. Of course, this is just a tiny slice of what sets this generation apart. Check out Appendix B (and www.iLifers.com) for more information about iLifers. The Appendix covers iLifers' unique take on the workplace, civic engagement, education, diversity and global citizenship.

For now, we'll focus on the iLifer character trait most directly related to *The $15,000 Year*.

iLifers and Money

According to the media, iLifers are financially astute and financially aloof, obsessed with money and nonchalant about it, impulse shoppers and well-researched consumers, wealthy and broke, frivolous spendthrifts and value-conscious savers and forthcoming and tight-lipped about money.

So, the pundits have really struggled to understand young people's fiscal dispositions. But, no worries, one of the purposes of this book is to provide a clear and definitive account of iLifers' spending habits and financial management behavior based on consumer expenditure surveys, market research and federal statistics that track income, savings, debt and investments. Section II and Section III offer detailed descriptions about how iLifers manage and spend their money (and how they can save) but, for now, here are a few facts to keep in mind:

Spending and Saving

According to the U.S. Bureau of Labor Statistics 2007 Consumer Expenditure Survey, the average consumer unit* under the age of 25 had an income of $30,802 after taxes. Of this, those under the age of 25 had an average of $29,457† in annual consumer expenditures. That means the average iLifer is spending more than 95 percent of his net income on direct *out-of-pocket* expenditures (i.e., housing, food, transportation, apparel, entertainment, education and other products and services). These out-of-pocket expenditures do not include student loan payments, retirement investments, or charitable giving. When these are added, the iLifer savings rate is much closer to zero and is negative in many cases.

Saddled with record amounts of student and consumer debt, iLifers represent the most indebted generation of young people in American history and many aren't too sure what to do about it.

*A consumer unit is defined by the BLS as "All members of a particular household who are related by blood, marriage, adoption or other legal arrangements" or, more relevant to iLifers, "a person living alone or sharing a household with others... but who is financially independent."

†Those with college degrees tend to earn and spend about 30 percent more than the average consumer, according to the BLS. This means the average college-educated iLifer unit is earning about $40,000 and spending close to 38,500 each year.

iLIFERS AND ENTREPRENEURSHIP

Dropping out of the corporate workforce to pursue entrepreneurship has become highly attractive option for today's young adults, half of which list "owning my own business" as a goal. We've come of age hearing stories of young entrepreneurs who dropped out of school or quit their entry-level jobs and went on to start multibillion-dollar companies. The Zuckerburgs, the Gateses, the Jobses, and a host of other famed entrepreneurial rock stars that many of us began wishing to emulate after our dreams of being the next Jordan or Spice Girl puttered out during a failed high school tryout or an embarrassing talent show performance. The result: For the first time in history, 18- to 24-year-olds are starting companies at a faster rate than 35- to 44-year-olds, according to a 2007 study by the Global Entrepreneurship Monitor.

The only business environment we've known is one where it is possible to quickly launch a business venture with minimal upfront costs, low operating expenses, scalability and, most importantly, no permission from traditional gatekeepers. In today's business world, democratizing technology has made it possible for young entrepreneurs, entertainers and e-capitalists to promote their products directly to consumers without appealing to the middlemen who controlled industries such as music and information technology in the past. Innovative ideas and products that may have died in their infancy 35 years ago because a vice president, publisher or A&R did not find them "groovy" enough, today have the opportunity to reach global audiences without gatekeeper support.

> *"While a kid 30 years ago might have been able to invent a new whirligig, the Internet era has given rise to something new; a cadre of really young kids whose innovations have had global impact. So, even if there aren't more young entrepreneurs than there used to be, they are capable, more than any young generation in the past, of reshaping the global economy. The age of gerontocracy is over."*
>
> —JOHN PALFREY AND URS GASSER, *Born Digital* (2008)

See Chapter 6 for more information about the $15,000 Year and entrepreneurship.

iLIFERS, DEBT AND FINANCIAL LITERACY

According to Nellie Mae, the average college student owns four credit cards and has accumulated $2,864 in consumer debt by the time he graduates. While this number has more than doubled during the past decade, it pales in comparison to amount of money iLifers owe to the new king of youth debt—the student loan. Because tuition and fees have been rising by record amounts in recent years (up more than 60 percent since 2001), current students can expect to graduate from college with an average of about $21,000 in loans, almost double what a student graduating in the mid-1990s borrowed.

Despite the extraordinary amount of borrowing now required to finance a college education (and despite iLifers' high-tech approach to financial management), the vast majority of students report feeling unprepared to manage their finances after graduation. This finding, from a 2008 Opinion Research Corporation survey, is supported by the following statistics:

- Only 5 percent of graduating college students consider themselves very knowledgeable about money management and investing, according the 2008 Millennium Generation Studies survey by Northwestern Mutual Financial Network.
- Only 18 percent young adults consider their financial physique to be "toned and fit." More than half (55 percent) describe their financial health as "a little flabby" and 27 percent say it's "seriously out of shape," according to the 2009 Young Adults & Money survey conducted by Lieberman Research Worldwide.
- In a 2008 financial literacy test administered by the Jump$tart Coalition, college seniors scored an average of 65 percent.
- The number of 18- to 24-year-olds declaring bankruptcy has increased 96 percent in the last 10 years.
- Most students did not attend high schools where personal finance education was a part of the curriculum. In Jump$tart's 2008 high school quiz, the average graduating senior answered just 48 percent of financial literacy questions correctly*.

iLifers' rocky relationship with money effectively became more tenuous when the financial systems collapsed in 2008. Most of us weren't heavily invested in the stock market or stuck with subprime mortgages but we felt the shockwaves of the downturn through job losses, wage cuts and tightened lending standards. More importantly, the fact that the first major economic crisis of iLifers' lives happened to be one of the worst the country has ever experienced has had a major psychological impact on the iLifer consumer.

Because the majority of your life will take place after this recession, how you choose to spend, save, borrow and invest your money will play a major role in determining what kind of financial actor you become in the short and long terms.

That's where *The $15,000 Year* comes into play.

This book offers a contemporary strategy for achieving the type of enduring financial security that will allow you to ride out this recession, improve your future standard of living and, possibly, change the world (before age 30).

*Down by more than 10 points since 1997, this was the lowest score recorded in the survey's history.

I.

CHAPTER 1

Riding Out the Recession: The $15,000 Year.

"So, how exactly do you 'ride out' a recession?"

Glad you asked.

The $15,000 Year is a unique, modern and aggressive strategy to help you *carpe* your financial security—and do so quickly. If you owe thousands in credit card debt and student loans, were a victim of the recession (e.g., lost a job, couldn't find one), or simply want to retire early, you're a perfect candidate for the $15,000 Year. This book will help you reduce "consumer expenditures" by as much as $15,000 this year and show you the best options for using this extra cash:

- **CREATE AN EMERGENCY SAVINGS FUND….** The Consumer Federation recently found that those under the age of 25 are the least likely to have money saved in the case of an emergency such as job loss or a sudden illness. (See Chapter 2.)
- **PAY DOWN STUDENT AND CONSUMER DEBT….** Today's students leave college deeper in debt than any previous generation and studies have shown a direct relationship between student debt and reduced homeownership among young adults. (See Chapter 3.)
- **FUND AN ENTREPRENEURIAL PROJECT…** Thanks to digital technology, starting a business (or producing an album, short film or book) has never been easier, less expensive or more exciting. But, in

order to do this, you'll probably need some startup capital. Sixty percent of young people list "lack of capital" as the main barrier to realizing their entrepreneurial aspirations. (See Chapter 6.)

- PAY YOURSELF TO TAKE A PERSONALLY FULFILLING AND SOCIALLY VALUABLE JOB.... The economic downturn has encouraged more college seniors to pursue less lucrative positions that allow them to give back. A 2009 survey by employment consultant Universum USA found that public service is now the top choice for employment after graduation. (See Chapter 5.)
- PUT MONEY AWAY FOR RETIREMENT.... A 2006 employee benefits study found that only 32 percent of young workers are participating in their employer's 401(k) plan (compared to 70 percent of those over 30). (See Chapter 4.)
- LIVE ON LESS UNTIL THE JOB MARKET REBOUNDS.... The unemployment rate for young Americans stood at 13 percent in early 2009 and iLifers* faced one of the most challenging job markets in recent history.
- AND MORE.... (Keep reading.)

Citing iLifer spending statistics from the 2007 Consumer Expenditure Survey for housing, transportation, food, entertainment and apparel (and providing savings tips in each of these areas), this book will show you exactly where you will need to cut back in order to save $15,000. The personal finance section will show you how to allocate these funds in ways that will boost your credit score, secure your future and (eventually) let you move out of your parents' house.

Top 6 Reasons to Save $15K This Year

6.
THE RISKS WILL NEVER BE LOWER. YOU WILL NEVER BE FREER.

Think about it. You're young, independent and you have no family to feed. Whatever audacious choices you make (e.g., going car-free, taking a pay cut to work in the Third World, investing 95 percent of your life savings in your first startup) will affect you and *only* you.

Your financial profile will never be less complicated and your liabilities will never be as few as they are now. Most likely, you have no mortgage to pay down, no life insurance premium to worry about and no college tuition funds to invest in.

*See Prologue for a definition of iLifers

When you're 35 years old with a mortgage to refinance, children to clothe and a slew of bills to manage, you probably won't be able to assume some of the risks that you are completely free to take on now. When you have a family of your own, putting all your savings into a business venture or quitting your corporate job to work for a fledgling nonprofit in India might be seen as irresponsible, not inspirational.

> Note: If you're a recent grad, you've already been living like a student—eating pizza, sleeping in a cell and paying zero dollars for music and movies—for the last four (or five) years. What's two more semesters?

5.
THE PAYOFFS WILL NEVER BE HIGHER.

- By paying off that $2,000 credit card debt in 12 weeks, instead of 12 months (or 12 years), you'll save hundreds of dollars by avoiding interest payments and improving your credit score. If you take this year to escape the debt trap in your 20s, statistics show you'll have a much higher chance of becoming a homeowner before age 30.
- If you start investing for retirement now—instead of waiting until mid-life—you could retire 10 years earlier (or a million dollars richer) than the average American due to the power of compound interest. (See Chapter 4.)
- Starting a business when you have three-quarters of your life ahead of you (rather than two-thirds or one-half) will give you a competitive advantage over the long term. Since iLifers show the highest propensity for serial entrepreneurship, this could be your opportunity to get the type of head start that will help you run your second, third and fourth startups successfully.

4.
EVERYBODY'S DOING IT.

What better reason is there than a little peer pressure? The downturn has made frugality popular and everyone—from the Richistani to the nouveau poor—is cutting back. According to a recent Gallup / USA Today poll, those 18 to 29 are the most likely to report saving now more than ever before (44 percent).

> *"Defying the stereotype of young spendthrifts, the 20-somethings surveyed said they're eating out less (62%), shopping recreationally less (73%), trying to save more (52%) and changing vacation plans (47%). Making better choices about money was ranked as the most important issue for individuals to consider today (52%)."*
>
> —MARY PILON for the Wall Street Journal, *Young People Freaked Out by the Market Act Accordingly*, April 3, 2009

3.

IT'S NEVER BEEN EASIER. *HINT: YOU HAVE THE CHEAT-BOOK IN YOUR HANDS.*

Today, saving money is not about depriving yourself of life's luxuries—it's about stretching your dollar as far as possible and paying the lowest price on the market for traditionally expensive goods and services (or getting them for free). As you'll see in Section III, technology is your best friend in this regard. Save $900 by cancelling your cable subscription and watch all your favorite shows online; cut $1,450 from your annual food bill by having personalized deals and coupons sent to your email account; use websites like www.retailmenot.com to save an extra 30 percent or more on apparel purchases and car rentals. The proliferation of techno-capital, or the cost-cutting power of technology, has completely changed the structure of the marketplace and, whether you know it or not, your $800 laptop is a virtual goldmine. This book shows you how to mine it.

2.

PUT THE MONEY IN THE BANK, AND NOBODY GETS HURT.

iLifers will *not* ruin the economy by significantly reducing their spending for a year. Yes, consumer spending makes up about 70 percent of America's economic activity—but, according to data from the Bureau of Labor Statistics, the under-25 set is responsible for only four percent of this spending. The broader economy will barely notice your spending slowdown, as the effect will be negligible.

In fact, by saving money now, you will most likely *help* the economic situation in the short term (next five years) and the long term (next 50 years). By the time you reach your late 20s and early 30s, you will be part of an age group that accounts for closer to 20 percent of American spending. Climbing out of debt in your 20s will give you the freedom to spend more liberally when it matters—to become the homeowner who can afford to pay his mortgage, the philanthropist who funds community cultural centers or the businesswoman who doesn't need to ask the government for a bailout.

1.
CHANGE THE WORLD.

In a recent *NEED* magazine interview, Nobel Peace Prize winner Muhammad Yunus encouraged the next generation of young people to sit down and type up a description of the kind of world they'd like to create. What would be the features of this world and what would its people be like? What kind of social order would prevail and how would the cultural and political landscapes look?

For Yunus, who wrote *Creating A World Without Poverty*, such a world would be free of deprivation, socially innovative and permanently peaceful.

Think about it for a second.

Your world might be characterized by equal opportunities for all, environmental sustainability, universal human rights or unwavering financial security. It might be free of political corruption, corporate irresponsibility, disease and hunger.

You'll read a lot in the pages ahead about coupon codes, dollar stretching and credit scores—but those are all means, not ends. At its core, the $15,000 Year is about promoting social equality, environmental awareness, good global citizenship, civic engagement, volunteering, charitable giving and other forms of social action that the world sorely needs in the 21st century.

By following the tips in the following chapters, you will be reducing the rate at which you consume the planet's scarce resources, rejecting the negativities of consumerism (in favor of helping others) and calling for social responsibility from the companies you do business with.

You will also have the opportunity to pay yourself with the money you'll be saving and break free from the work-and-spend merry-go-round that so many are too afraid or self-conscious to abandon. Once you've escaped this cycle, you'll have the freedom to take a position (or start a business) that creates real meaning in the world or in other people's lives.

There are plenty of reasons for saving $15K this year, but they all will help you take a crucial first step towards gaining the financial, psychological and occupational freedom that will allow you to achieve your individual goals and advance the collective good of society.

The majority of iLifers' lives will take place after this recession and, after all the dust settles, this generation will be responsible for steering the country through the 21st century. At the end of the day, what the world looks like in 2050 and what the history eBooks say about this century will be a result of what this generation does (or does not do).

Throughout the book, you'll come across commentary that relates the $15,000 Year to the "Changing the World" theme and lets you know exactly how to make an impact while seizing your financial security at the same time.

> *"What will happen over the course of their lives is, of course, unknowable. But in all likelihood, the Millennial Generation will dominate the story of the twenty-first century to much the same degree as the World War II-winning G.I. Generation dominated the story of the twentieth."*
>
> —WILLIAM STRAUSS AND NEIL HOWE, *Millennials Rising* (2000)

On Structure

The rest of the book is separated into two parts.

Section II (Chapters 2 through 6) outlines various options for putting the saved money to use for you and your future. In Chapter 2, on savings, you'll find out how to create the perfect, post-recession emergency fund. Chapter 3 offers information about debt repayment (i.e., credit cards and student loans). Chapter 4 is about investing for the future (e.g., retirement), Chapter 5 covers work-life and Chapter 6 is all about the $15,000 Year and entrepreneurship.

Section III (Chapters 7 through 12) provides the nitty gritty of exactly what you will need to do to save $15K this year. Chapter 7 goes through the setup process—how to start the 12-month program—with information about creating, understanding and following your budget (yeah, the boring stuff, but extremely necessary and useful). Chapter 8 takes you through the largest expenditure for most Americans—Housing—and shows you how to significantly reduce your one-year bill in this area. This chapter covers leasing your first apartment, furnishing your pad, saving on utilities and more. Chapter 9 takes on the second largest expenditure: Transportation. From purchasing a used car to saving on gas and air travel, this chapter gets you from point A to point B on the cheap. Chapter 10 focuses on the last of the Big Three: Food. It's a 21st century guide to cooking, eating out and grocery shopping on a tight budget. Chapter 11 is full of tips on how to save on Entertainment (from movies to travel to cell phone services). Last but not least, Chapter 12, on Apparel, will have you rockin' the latest looks for less.

THE $15K YEAR-LITE

If drastic circumstances make it impossible for you to reduce expenditures by $15,000 this year (e.g., you just had triplets), don't worry. The tips in this book will help you save whatever amount you want ($5,000, $7,500). If you don't yet have a steady income, try to live on a *maximum* budget of $15,000 this year. And even if you're fortunate enough not to need to cut back at all, this book is full of personal finance tips that will help you make smart financial decisions.

II.

CHAPTER 2

SAVINGS.

Most of your elders wish they could simply go back in time and do it all over again.

The voices warning them about the possibility of a financial system meltdown like we experienced in 2008 and 2009 were few and far between (and mostly soft-spoken) in the boom years of the 1990s and 2000s and those beckoning them to spend, enjoy and live life to the fullest were louder and more enticing than ever. In their postwar youths, America was the epitome of prosperity and the Joneses had decided that they'd be damned if anyone actually caught up to them. Luxury products infiltrated mainstream society as modern suburbanization dawned with all kinds of new status dynamics and no one wanted to be left behind. The American Dream could now be ordered up on credit and, besides, everyone was doing it.

So they spent.

During their lifetimes, they've seen the national savings rate plummet from a solid 11.2 percent in 1982 to a troubling -1.1 percent in 2006*. The average home size grew 66 percent between 1970 and 2005 and the average amount spent on cars by middle-income Americans

*The lowest rate since the Great Depression.

doubled between 1984 and 2005. By 2008, the average adult was charging $15,000 on his credit card each year.

When the financial markets collapsed in 2008, their combination of lackadaisical saving and high debt left them defenseless as foreclosures, layoffs and a crashing stock market brought the economy to a halt.

Ask them what ever happened to that ever so important consumer item they just had to have—the Laserdisc player or DeLorean they depleted their savings accounts to get or the collection of bell bottoms they went deep into debt to buy—and most will draw a blank. Many cringe to think about the money they've given away to credit card companies and financiers in the form of interest payments simply because they could not delay gratification.

But hindsight, of course, is 20/20. It's easy to look back at an older generation and point the finger and criticize its members for lacking prudence or restraint. What's more difficult (and much less popular) is looking forward and avoiding the same stumbling blocks that others faced before you.

And today it's more difficult than ever.

In the 21st century, you have more reasons than any previous generation to go down the dangerous path of overspending and debt that many of our parents walked. Here's why:

Between 1983 and 1995—the prime childhood years of iLifers—the number of marketing dollars targeted to reach children rose exponentially, from $100 million to $1 billion per year, priming you for a life of consumerism before you knew any better. Today, there are more corporations trying to win your loyalty than there have ever been, more marketing messages saturating your environment than ever before and more luxury items for the taking than history has ever known. Getting your hands on a credit card is as simple as it's ever been—sign up at a ball game or at the airport or in front of the campus bookstore (they'll even toss in a free mug or t-shirt). Of course, credit card companies make sure the instruction manual (if there is one) is written with fine print and obscure language.

With tuition costs up more than 250 percent since 1976 and the rate of student borrowing more than double what it was just a decade ago, you're already starting your adult life much more indebted than previous cohorts of young Americans. Despite this sharp increase in the cost of higher education, financial literacy education in our high schools and universities remains painfully underemphasized. Less than 30 percent of high school students are given the opportunity to take even a week's worth of course work in money management and very few colleges have incorporated personal finance courses into their core curricula.

According to the Federal Reserve's 2007 Survey of Consumer Finances, the average iLifer's net worth has been on the decline for the past few years. Between 2004 and 2007, the median net worth increased for all family-structure groups *except* iLifers (or, in the language of the Fed, "younger single families without children").

This is just a small slice of the evidence that shows iLifers represent the most leveraged generation of young people in history while simultaneously being the most at risk to spend outside of its means. Throw in the fact that we are coming of age during a recession that saw more than 5 million people lose their jobs and the national debt grow to more than $11 trillion and you have a pretty troubling situation.

Needless to say, the financial odds are stacked against you.

That's where this book comes in. There are a number of ways you can spend the extra $15,000 (as you will see in the rest of this section) but using it to establish some financial stability—and to do so quickly—is probably the most effective and valuable option for the iLifer looking to avoid the same kind of financial roller coaster that the many Americans found themselves strapped into in 2008 and 2009.

Create an emergency savings fund, quickly eliminate student loan debt with rapid-repayment on steroids or pay off the balances on those high-interest credit cards and take control of your FICO score before it takes control of you. There are so many better alternatives to spending frivolously to buy many of the things that, with a little effort, you could pick up for a reduced price thanks to the democratization of the 21st century marketplace.

In this section, you will learn how delaying gratification for just one year will allow you to live at a much higher standard of living in the future and hedge yourself against the type of fiscal downturns that tend to demoralize the unprepared. Let's start with a little history.

Personal Savings Rate

The U.S. personal savings rate, or the percentage of a person's disposable income that they save, has basically nose-dived during the past 30 years, falling by more than 80 percent since 1981. By 2006, the average American was spending more than she earned. For the past few years, our personal savings rate has hovered around 0 percent, ranking America dead last among all industrialized nations (Japan, China and Germany, for instance, have had savings rates in the double digits for years). For some perspective, the 2004 U.S. savings rate of 0.2 percent means Americans with salaries of $40,000 put away only about $1.50 every week.

GRAPH 1: U.S. PERSONAL SAVINGS RATE, 1949–2006

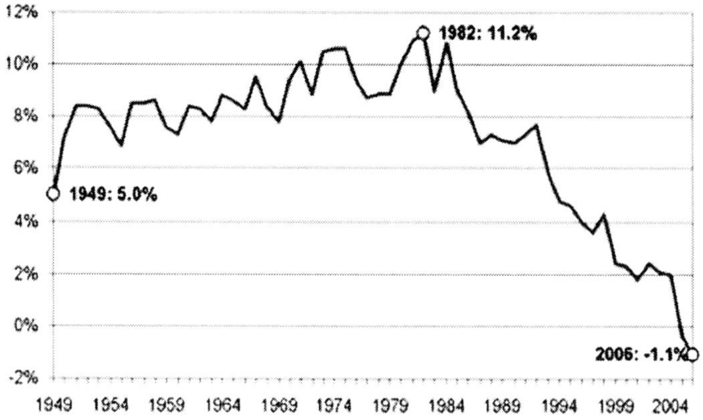

Source: Bureau of Economic Analysis, National Income and Product Accounts, Table 2.1, Personal Income and Its Disposition.

Most economists agree that this simply cannot continue if the United States is to remain a financially secure nation in the future. After the worst housing bust in history and the most severe financial system collapse since the Great Depression, it has become crystal clear that putting away such a small portion of our incomes is not sustainable. (Some economists argue that the low savings rate is one of the ingredients that helped sustain the 2008 recession into 2009. As markets fell, consumer confidence plummeted and many chose not to spend because they had so little saved away in case they lost their jobs or their money in the stock market.) Because the recession was so deep and far-reaching, Americans learned that relying on increasing home values and stock market wealth while saving little or nothing was a recipe for turmoil.

THE $15,000 YEAR ENDORSES... Savings Rehab...

You're young and the savings rate you establish for yourself now will play a major role in determining what your future financial profile looks like. It will determine when you can retire, when you can buy a house, if you can start a business and whether or not you can send your kids to the colleges of their choice. Saving 15 grand this year will give you a solid savings rate and set a valuable precedent for future saving.

Let's say you majored in chemical engineering in college—and you were fortunate enough to get or keep a job during the recession. If reported average salaries for entry-level employees can be trusted, conservatively we can say that you'll be making somewhere in the range of $45,000 a year after taxes, most likely more. For you, doing the $15,000 Year would require a savings rate of about 33 percent. Put that figure next to the national average and it may seem a little extreme. But that's the point. Along with all the other benefits of taking a year of reduced consumption, you get a hard-core, Rocky-IV-type training in savings rate management. After the year is over, you'll have no trouble maintaining a respectable double-digit savings rate during the rest of your Independent Life Stage, and hopefully, for the next 30 years or so until you retire (early and on your own accord).

For those of you with a less lucrative job than Mr. Engineering-major, your savings rate will be even higher*—if you make $35,000 a year, we're talking in the 40 percent range. Any money "expert" will tell you that it's unrealistic. But it's been done before. No doubt, it will take some strategizing and good deal of restraint, but remember:

1. **It's only a year.** Think about how fast senior year flew by. It'll be over before you know it.
2. **Saving $15K has never been easier or more appropriate in modern history.** It's a recession!
3. **Being in the black is apparently the new black.** Everybody's doing it—the savings rate has been trending upwards recently (around 5 percent as of Q1 2009) and many economists believe that

*If you're unemployed, you won't have such a high savings rate—but you'll still learn how to live on less. Once you land a job and a steady paycheck, your savings rate will shoot up.

this financial downturn will leave a lasting impression on the psyche of the American consumer, leading to a long-lasting increase in the savings rate. Some envision the U.S. moving much closer to its historical average of 7 percent for the foreseeable future.

4. **This book will show you how.** Section III is full of tips on how to save money in the key areas of housing, transportation, food, entertainment, apparel and communication.

5. **The payoffs over the long term can be massive.** As you will see in the following pages, when it comes to financial security, peace of mind and retirement, there's nothing like money in the bank.

Creating a Post-Recession Emergency Fund

A second, and more immediate, savings-related reason for the $15,000 Year is the suddenly popular emergency savings fund. If you're like me, you went through most of your life with no one telling you anything about this very basic account that every financial adviser calls the foundation of a stable financial portfolio. If you've never heard the term "emergency fund" or any of its synonyms before, you should probably be a little upset that you were shorted by the establishment. But, not to worry, you've come to the right place.

THE $15,000 YEAR ENDORSES... Stepping Your Emergency Game Up... (Peace of Mind: Priceless.)

Studies show that young people are highly unlikely to have a significant amount of money put aside for an emergency. Even older adults are slacking in this category. According to a 2007 survey by the Consumer Federation of America, only 40 percent of adults have a separate account for emergency expenses. Those under the age of 24 (and those with incomes of $25,000 or less) are the least likely to save, the survey found.

WHAT IS IT?

An emergency fund is simple. It's money saved up for the type of unexpected, money-devouring event that happens to everybody (e.g., you have a serious medical issue, your car breaks down or you get laid off and your income stream dries up). When life happens, your emergency fund is supposed to come to your rescue and keep you from flipping out or making financially dangerous decisions.

THE PERFECT EMERGENCY FUND...

1. Amounts to somewhere between three and nine months worth of your minimum living expenses. Based on federal statistics, if you're like the average under-25 iLifer with a bachelor's degree, you usually spend about $2,550 a month on expenditures such as rent, utilities, food, car payments and entertainment. Assuming you would cut back a little if you lost your income, this means your post-recession emergency fund should *ideally* be somewhere in the range of $5,000 to $10,000.
2. Is money that is highly liquid, which means it's available immediately, or almost immediately. When an emergency or unforeseen event that challenges your financial stability comes up, you should be able to access this money quickly, easily and without penalty.
3. Is kept in a high-yield savings account. Since this money will (hopefully) be sitting on emergency standby for many years, you want it to grow as quickly as possible. Your local bank, an online savings account, a certificate of deposit (CD) or a money market account are all options.
    a. You can shop for the best CDs and money market accounts at www.bankrate.com.

       NOTE: The CDs with the best rates come with a few stipulations. Usually, you have to deposit a minimum amount in order to open them. This can range from a few hundred bucks to tens of thousands of dollars but you can expect to see $2,500 to $5,000 in minimum deposit requirements.

WHAT IT AIN'T

An emergency fund is not money for a new dress-shoes-purse combo for a date with Mr. Maybe Right. It's not "Happy-Birthday-To-Me" money. It's not "This new rug doesn't match my furniture so time to buy new a living room set" money. It's not "My girlfriend will leave me if I don't get her an awesome jewel this V-Day" money. While all of these scenarios may seem like emergencies at the time, when a real emergency comes up (e.g., you lose your job), you'll probably wish you hadn't cried wolf for Mr. Definitely Wrong.

WHY IS IT SO IMPORTANT?

Stashing so much cash in a savings account when you could be taking a really nice vacation, buying a 60-inch flatscreen or even investing for the future may not seem like the most exciting or youthful idea. After all, a wisely invested $10,000 can turn into a cool quarter million by the time you're ready to retire and the interest from a savings account would barely cover the cost of inflation. Here's why this makes sense:

First, an emergency fund gives you priceless peace of mind. Once you have this account established, you can live without much of the financial stress that most families experience when a child gets sick or rumors of impending layoffs infiltrate the workplace. The 2008 downturn made it clear that job risk is a serious threat and job stability is never guaranteed regardless of industry, position, tenure or perceived indispensability. Of the 5 million people who lost their jobs between January 2008 and March 2009, at least 2 million did not have a separate account with money put away for emergency purposes. Hundreds of thousands more didn't have enough saved away to get them through their period of unemployment.

Second, because of its liquidity, an emergency fund trumps any other form of long-term savings in the case of unforeseen financial challenges. The costs of taking on consumer debt, dipping into your retirement savings or selling off other investments are incredibly high and the time it takes to access tied-up assets can exacerbate problems when you're in a bind.

HOW THE $15,000 YEAR WILL GET YOU THERE

Most personal finance books will tell you to stash away $50 here and there until you have a decent emergency fund. This is a fine strategy for those who like the thrill of being on an unpredictable and shoddy financial roller coaster. But that's not you and the 2008–2009 economic recession has made it clear that being noncommittal about saving is a recipe for future trouble.

My problem with the 50-bucks-or-whatever-you-can-manage-at-the-end-of-the-month strategy is that it's far too slow to serve its original purpose of creating peace of mind. Now that we know just how volatile the stock and job markets can be, having an emergency fund and having one now is more important than ever. Here's what I mean:

Even if you diligently saved $80 every month, it would take you almost 10 years to save up $10,000, assuming you had an emergency-free decade and you never had to take money out of the fund (no one's that lucky, btw). That's a long time to wait, holding onto the hope that an unexpected tide doesn't wash away your savings sandcastle as you slowly pile on each teaspoon of sand.

I thought the idea of this was to eliminate stress. That sounds dreadful.

Even worse, think about the fact that even if you made it through the 10-year period financially unscathed and arrived at 2020 with a nice emergency fund of $10K, by then it probably would not be enough to cover your new monthly expenses for more than a couple months if you lost your job or got sick. According the 2007 Consumer Expenditure Survey by the Bureau of Labor Statistics (BLS), the average mid-30s household has monthly out-of-pocket expenditures of about $4,435 (excluding taxes, investments, credit card bills, etc.). That total is 31 percent higher for people with bachelor's degrees (about $5,800).

To put some context to all these numbers, let's press fast-forward and take a look at your life 10 years from now: You just moved into your first home, a 3-bedroom beauty, with your loving spouse and brilliant kid (total housing costs: $1,500 monthly, according to BLS). You're thrilled that your four-year-old, Junior, can speak three languages (private pre-school tuition: $750 monthly). You also just bought a new, completely electric, fully-equipped SUV that drives itself (car payments and maintenance: $550 per month). Add your food bill ($550) and you're already up to $3,350 in monthly outlays and you still haven't paid for many of your expenses (e.g., insurance, cell phone, credit cards, entertainment).

The main point is that, as you begin to settle into adult life in the post-recession world, taking the slow, Sisyphus-like approach to building your emergency fund could land you and your family on a one- or two-month path to bankruptcy (or worse) if, God forbid, an emergency wiped out your income. Why would anyone advise this?

Besides having pre-recession training, the other main reason financial advisors suggest such a lackluster approach to building emergency savings is because their books and TV shows tend to be directed at older people who have grown so accustomed to living with such a low personal savings rate that the idea putting away more than an extra $10 or $20 a week would probably scare them away from the concept all together. They have established such financially complicated lifestyles and tight budgets that building an emergency fund has to take a backseat to the line of mortgages, credit card bills, life insurance premiums, tuition payments and other financial priorities they have locked themselves into.

As a young person with relatively few obligations (no mortgage, no children to feed, etc.), you have the freedom and flexibility to take the fast track to financial security. This is a prime opportunity for you to establish a solid emergency fund foundation in less than 12 months, not 10 years. It's a chance to seize the kind of peace of mind that will allow you to live a full and complete life free of the type of financial worries that many Boomers experienced during the recession as they saw their retirement wealth fade into thin air.

Using the savings tips and guidelines in this book, take $3,000 or $5,500 or however much money you need to feel comfortable in the event of an unexpected drain on your finances and invest it in a *separate* account (for emergencies only). Then, as they say, go forth in peace.

You may not know what it's like to have more than $1,000 in your account and you may have always considered The Bank of Mom & Dad to be your emergency plan. But, as someone who has been on both sides of the emergency fence (not having a fund during a summer internship housing dilemma in 2007 and having a fund during the recession in 2009), I can honestly tell you that it really is the difference between having an anxiety attack and serenely saying "This too shall pass," as you check your CD balance online and realize you'll be just fine. And there's absolutely nothing like that feeling of peace in the midst of mayhem.

Having a solid emergency fund in your early- or mid-20s will put you way ahead of the game in this respect. As it grows, it can become more than simply a resource in the time of tragedy. A four- or five-figure emergency fund can double as a springboard into occupational freedom. It might allow you to leave an unfulfilling job and pursue an interest or to take a six-month leave and write a book. It might let you take advantage of an opportunity to go abroad and work pro bono for a couple months or take an extended maternity leave. It might let you go full time with the blog you started as a hobby when your readership starts to take off.

CHAPTER 3

DEBT.

> *"This generation of twentysomethings is straining under the weight of college loans and other debt, a crushing load that separates it from every previous generation."*
>
> —MINDY FETTERMAN AND BARBARA HANSEN FOR USA TODAY
> *YOUNG PEOPLE STRUGGLE TO DEAL WITH KISS OF DEBT*
> NOVEMBER 22, 2006

Credit Cards

Naturally, while the personal savings rate was plummeting between the early '80s and early 2008, the total amount of consumer debt was soaring. Americans bought what they wanted, charging those things that they couldn't afford and not thinking too much of it.

As a result, the size of America's total consumer debt grew nearly five times over between 1980 ($355 billion) and 2001 ($1.7 trillion). In 2009, consumer debt stood in excess of $2.6 trillion (about $8,500 per person). Revolving credit such as credit card debt makes up about 40 percent of this total and America's love affair with plastic has never been more sensuous. The stats are staggering:

- Americans own approximately 1.4 billion credit cards, averaging nearly nine cards per cardholder.
- Consumers were expected to charge $2.7 trillion to their credit cards in 2010, more than $15,000 per cardholder.
- In 2006, Americans carried approximately $886 billion in credit card debt (that number is expected to grow to $1.09 trillion by the year 2010). This comes out to about than $5,500 in credit card debt per cardholder. The average household carried more than $8,500 in credit card debt.

- Between 2000 and 2006, even as real income was more or less stagnant, credit card borrowing increased by about 30 percent.
- In 2008, more than 1 million people filed for consumer bankruptcy, an increase of more than 30 percent over 2007. The number in 1980? About 300,000.

iLifers and Consumer Debt

While most young people have less consumer debt and fewer credit cards (2.8) than the average American, iLifers are much deeper in debt than any previous generation of 20-somethings.

The average college student has received dozens of solicitations for credit cards and escapes campus with a balance of $2,864 at graduation. After college, this amount increases as young recent graduates now carry an average balance of more than $4,000 in credit card debt, representing a 55 percent increase since 1992.

As an iLifer, you are at a credit crossroads and the path you decide to take will basically determine whether you end up living your life submerged under the tide of credit card debt or become one of those envied people with flawless credit profiles. But staying out of the consumer debt trap has become harder than ever for young adults. Banks, lenders and other purveyors of plastic have taken advantage of young people's financial inexperience, making shady partnerships with universities and strategically targeting iLifers with high-interest student cards and aggressive marketing ploys. Because the cost of higher education is at an all-time high, most students sign up for cards to cover their expenses, not realizing that they will probably end up paying much more than they bargained for when all is said and done.

While these credit card companies, who descend on campuses every fall like vultures, should be ashamed of themselves, the good news is that the level of credit card debt for the graduating iLifer is still relatively low, when compared to older cardholders. It is also quite manageable, if you keep in mind that marriage, children and homeownership most likely won't come along for a few years.

THE $15,000 YEAR ENDORSES... Controlling Your Consumer Debt Before it Controls You.

One of the purposes of this book is to encourage you to take advantage of this unique life stage you find yourself in, pay off your consumer debt in a matter of months and be on your way towards a debt-free life. Simple.

The $15,000 Year can be used as a strategy to face your credit consumer debt demons head on and grab your credit score by the horns early in the game before it goes rogue on you and takes over your life. Although there are tons of voices enticing you with sweet-sounding whispers to take the well-trodden path of excessive spending, the following pages will let you know that there is another way and it doesn't include living like a bum. Spending *wisely* is one of the themes endorsed by this book and, in Section III, you'll see exactly how to do that. For now, let's expose consumer debt and credit cards for the great American hoax they have become.

THE TRUTH ABOUT CREDIT CARDS

SCENARIO: You worked hard for four (or five) years, graduated and now you are ready to treat yourself. So you go out and buy a plasma TV or a new wardrobe and run up a balance of $2,000 on your credit card (which has a 19.8 percent interest rate). If you only pay the minimum each month (let's say 3 percent of total, or $60 at first), how long will it take to pay off the $2,000 balance, even if you never make another purchase?

A. 3 years and 8 months
B. 6 years and 1 month
C. 8 years and 11 months
D. 12 years and 6 months

The answer is D—12.583 years to be exact. That's right, more than a decade, assuming your payments are never late and you do not add any new purchases. By the time you finish, you will have paid interest in the amount of $2,065. To be clear, that's $2,000, *plus* another $2,065, for a *total* of $4,065. Even if you never used that card again, you paid more than twice the original amount for clothes you wore for only a year or a TV that you ended up selling for 300 bucks on Craigslist eighteen months after you bought it.

This is where credit card companies make their money. It's why they courted you so aggressively during your first weeks on campus as you tried to buy your books—offering free pizza, frequent flyer miles and t-shirts. It's why so many companies have "rewards" programs that give you bonuses for running up a high balance on your card. It's why the language used in describing your credit terms and conditions might as well be Latin.

> *"If you are a consumer of the 'preferred' or 'valued' customer type—that is, the type to max out cards and pay the minimum*

> *only (with the occasional late payment)—it is highly unlikely your consumer debt will ever be paid off. You will continue to pay this month for food you consumed years ago, clothes you've long since given away, and other stuff you've undoubtedly forgotten about completely. That, my friends, is perma-debt, and the credit-card companies love it."*
>
> —MARY HUNT, *The Complete Cheapskate* (2006)

Not only will using a credit card frivolously land you in permanent debt, it will screw up your FICO score (your credit rating), which ultimately determines if you will be able to buy a home, rent an apartment or get a car loan with a decent interest rate in the future. It may even affect your ability to land a job or rent a nice apartment.

WHAT TO DO ABOUT THE DEBT YOU HAVE NOW...

Take the appropriate portion of the $15,000 you will be saving, put it towards a rapid debt repayment plan and make sure these evil lenders don't see an additional shilling of your money.

There are various strategies out there for paying off all your debt and doing it wisely. Some personal finance experts say you should focus on paying off your card with the highest interest rate first, while paying only the minimums on all the others, and snowball it down until you've paid off all of your debt. Others say you should pay a single, flat amount (say, $125 a month) regardless of the declining minimum. With a debt of $5,000 and an interest rate of 15 percent, this strategy would get you out of debt in four years and eight months (as opposed to a repayment time of more than 20 years if you pay only the 2.5 percent minimum each month).

While this is fine strategy for people looking to get out of debt in a shorter than average amount of time, five years is still a long time and you'd still be paying a lot of interest for items long after you used them ($1,975 in the example above).

THE $15,000 YEAR ENDORSES... Paying Off All Your Consumer Debt in One Year... And then buying yourself something nice with the money you saved in avoided interest. For additional euphoria, pay for it with a fistful of cash.

With the $15,000 you will be saving ($1,250 per month), you can pay off the $5,000 debt from the example above in a matter of months.

For example, taking two thirds of those monthly savings (about $870) and using it to pay down that debt would have you debt-free in six months. The total interest you would have to pay would only be $221. If you took the four-years-and-eight-months method, you would end up paying $1,975 in interest. That's a difference of $1,761!

I know the idea of cutting back consumption by $15,000 may seem impossible, but, like I said before, a one-year investment of dedicated dollar stretching can lead to massive financial payoffs in the long term. I can't emphasize this enough. Think about the $1,700+ you would be saving, just by escaping future interest payments. Put that money to good use after the year is over and treat yourself to the sweetness of delayed gratification fulfilled.

The point of the $15,000 Year is to help you seize control of your finances—to get you off the American Express-way to bankruptcy and onto an accelerated track to consumer-debt-free living. As a young person relatively light on consumer debt (anything less than $3,000 is a lightweight amount, *relatively*) and low on major financial obligations (no, your tech gadget addiction or Coach bag obsession does not count as an obligation), this is probably the only time in your life when it will be possible to pay off your consumer debt in a matter of weeks, not years. Why not *carpe diem* and pull yourself out of the sticky sludge of indebtedness in record timing? Your FICO score will thank you.

> *"The average credit card indebted young adult household now spends nearly 24 percent of its income on debt payments."*
> —TAMARA DRAUT AND JAVIER SILVA, *Generation Broke: Growth of Debt Among Young Americans* (2004)

DEBT REPAYMENT CALCULATORS

Financial websites such as www.mint.com, www.consumercredit.com, and www.credit-cards.interest.com provide easy to use debt repayment calculators that can show you the best method for paying off your debt depending on your financial profile.

ALREADY OUT OF CREDIT CARD DEBT?

If you are fortunate enough to have made it this far without taking on substantial credit card debt, good for you. Pat yourself on the back. Get one or two credit cards and use them wisely, paying off the balances each month so you can establish some credit and reach FICO score nirvana. Live happily ever after.

But you're not off the hook yet. It's likely you have another source of debt that needs to be addressed. And, like all money that isn't yours, the sooner you give it back, the happier your life will be.

The $15,000 Year Takes on Student Loans

So we already know that today's iLifers are paying more for their education than any previous generation. To put some context to the statistic of a 250 percent rise in tuition cost during the last 30 years, let's take a look at what Baby Boomers and Gen-Xers spent and borrowed for higher education.

The average cost of tuition and fees at a public four-year college in the 1977–1978 school year was $2,225 (in 2007 dollars) compared to $6,185 in 2008. (For private universities, these numbers are $9,172 and $23,712, respectively.) More than two-thirds of today's college students have to take on debt for their education while less than half of graduates in 1993 had student loans, says the Project on Student Debt. Student borrowing has doubled over the past decade, with new student loans amounting to about $85 billion in 2008.

The average college senior can expect to graduate with more than $20,000 in student loans (closer to $25,000 for private universities) and those in graduate school can expect more than $50,000 in loans on commencement day.

If your student loan debt is anywhere near this $20,000 average, forget what your bank statement says. You have a negative amount of money. This bluntness is not intended to make you feel bad. But most people don't take their student loans seriously and, as a result, the already high cost of education increases significantly over time.

Most college grads end up paying for their education long after they've forgotten whatever they learned in that Intro to Art History class. Even at the relatively low interest rate of the popular subsidized Federal Stafford loan (6 percent, as of March 2009), if you take 15 years to pay off your $20,000 tab, you will end up paying more than $10,000 in interest.

That's a lot of money—but not too painful since the interest rate is much better than most credit cards and your education pays for itself many times over during the course of your lifetime. But a larger issue that should concern you is the sheer amount of your life you will spend paying for some kind of education.

Let's do the fast-forward thing again but now we'll put you in your late 30s. You've finally finished paying for your diploma. Hooray. Think you're done paying for education? Think again. Your polyglot preschooler has blossomed into a junior high whiz kid who's already thinking about college. If tuition and fees continue to rise at the current rates (twice the speed of inflation), it is quite possible you will be spending (or, more likely, *borrowing*), somewhere in the range of $25,000 to put Junior through a public university in a few years. Oh, and Junior has a bright younger sister who is a free spirit and is set on going to a liberal arts college where all students are required to create their own major. Even if her good grades and superb test scores land her a few nice scholarships, you can still expect her four-year private university studies to add an extra $50,000 to $60,000 to your lifetime education bill.

Because of soaring education costs, increased student borrowing and steadily growing rates of college enrollment, our generation is likely to be the first in American history to spend more than half of our lives indebted to an educational institution.

> *"The percentage of former students reporting that they would have borrowed less if they had to do it again increased from 31 percent in 1991, to 54 percent in 2002."*
>
> —Sandy Baum and Marie O'Malley, *College on Credit: How Borrowers Perceive Their Education Debt* (2003)

How you deal with your student debt will play a major role in determining your future standard of living. For example, Jennifer Shand's 2007 analysis of the Fed's Consumer Finance Survey found that "educational debt is associated with reduced homeownership rates for young households in recent years, and the effect is substantial." Basically, as the cost of education has risen, more young adults have had to delay homeownership because they're bogged down by student loans and other debt.

But that's not going to happen to you…

THE $15,000 YEAR ENDORSES… Paying Your Student Loans Off… Put college officially behind you and count this as one less bill you will get in the mail in future years.

One of the best things about student loans is that many of them give you a grace period before interest starts to accrue (usually six to nine months after graduation). This is perfect for recent grads looking to get maximum returns out of the $15K Year. After you've spent the first six months paying off your $3,000 credit card debt or establishing an emergency fund, turn your focus to knocking out a large chunk of your student debt in a short period of time.

For example, if you spend two-thirds of your $15,000 savings (or $10,000) and reduce your debt by half in your first year out of school, and then add just $150 each month in subsequent years, you can be debt-free before you turn 30, and you'd only end up paying about $2,500 in interest. That's about $7,500 less than what you would have paid if you had stuck with the 15-year payment plan above. Congrats. Go buy yourself a motorcycle.

THE iLIFER'S GUIDE TO TACKLING STUDENT DEBT

1. **Know what you owe.** Check the National Student Loan Data System's website at www.nslds.ed.gov for a list of all your loans along with their interest rates. Also get in touch with your school's financial aid office for personalized assistance.
2. **Know when your payments are due and how much they will be.** Put it on your Google Calendar or get a monthly alert by text or email from your budgeting site of choice. Late fees are very 20th Century.
3. **Develop a wise and realistic strategy for settling this debt.**
    a. Use a loan repayment calculator like the one at www.finaid.org. It'll tell you how much you should pay each month depending on how quickly you want to pay down your student debt. It will also let you know exactly how much interest you will be paying based on the repayment plan you choose.
    b. Make an informed decision about whether it is in your best interest to consolidate your loans. Websites like www.studentaid.ed.gov and www.smartmoney.com can help you determine if consolidation* is the appropriate route for you.
4. **Decide whether rapid repayment of this debt is the best use of your money.** Many personal finance experts say that student loan debt qualifies as "good debt," and therefore you

---

*Loan consolidation is the process of combining various loans into one massive new loan with a new interest rate.

shouldn't necessarily rush to pay it off with the same haste as high-interest debt such as credit cards. There are other financial investments, such as a Roth IRA or solid mutual fund, that might give you a better return for your money. I'll cover some of these options in the next chapter but check websites like www.young-money.com or www.20somethingfinance.com for great up to date information and testimonials.

CHAPTER 4

INVESTING FOR THE FUTURE.

Thanks to the swift advancement of medical science, increased early detection of disease and the growth of self-diagnosing via the Internet, iLifers can expect to live longer than any previous generation of Americans. That's great. It means we will be able to see our great-grandchildren grow up, ride in the first generation of flying cars and maybe even see the Cubs win a World Series (if we're lucky) before we kick ye ole bucket.

But it also means that, compared to our generational predecessors, we will have to think more seriously, more strategically and earlier on in life about how we will pay for our lengthy retirements.

Unlike our grandparents, we're basically on our own when it comes to financing our post-work periods. The Social Security system isn't looking too promising for those of us who will be retiring around 2050 and living for another quarter century or more after we leave the workforce. The system wasn't designed with such life expectancy trends in mind and the huge cohort of Boomers will soon be taking out a big chunk of what's left of the S.S. pie.

Another financial challenge we face in the future is the speedily rising national debt. To put it simply, our elders have borrowed mind-boggling amounts from us to sustain the government's record-high spending spree. The gross national debt stood at an eye-popping

$11 trillion in early 2009 and was expected to increase as the federal government planned to pump trillions of additional dollars into a cocktail of stimulus programs aimed at propping up the badly bruised economy. As the debt continues to rise at a record pace—it has doubled since 2000—the growing consensus is that the youngest generations (and those who will come after them) will be stuck with the bill. Some economists strongly believe that iLifers are likely to be the first generation in American history with a lower standard of living than their parents. Others argue that tax rates will have to more than double during our lifetimes in order for the country to get by. Some politicians and commentators have gone as far as calling the debt, which is growing by a billion dollars each day, "generational theft."

> *"On top of [students'] personal debts, each of them unknowingly bears more than $184,000 in federal liabilities and unfunded government promises. That's each American's individual share of over $10 trillion in public debt, plus $43 trillion in promised benefits for Social Security and Medicare, which in addition to other liabilities, brings our real national debt to a staggering $56.4 trillion. This level of indebtedness is simply unsustainable."*
>
> —WWW.INDEBTED.COM (2009)

That might have been tough to read but there's good news as well. Investing for the future is the best way to hedge yourself against economic stagnation and, because you're young, you're in the best position to take advantage of the power of compound interest and make a million bucks off your latte money.

THE $15,000 YEAR ENDORSES... Starting Early and Doing it Big... The Power of Compound Interest.

The $15K Year advocates a unique approach to investing for the future that combines the traditional advice of "starting early" with the under-recommended strategy of "starting big." While each of these approaches is quite powerful independently, their combined powers can be mind-blowing.

Most personal finance advisers emphasize the importance of starting early when investing for the future. They make it very clear that young people are at the best stage of their lives to save for the future and that it's all about the *length* of time invested. The time factor is so crucial because of a basic pecuniary principle called the "power of compound interest." Here's a brief example to illustrate what this is:

Let's say we have two iLifers, Aaron and Zach—both 22 years old. They both have an extra $300 each month to invest or spend as they please. Aaron chooses to invest his money into a retirement account that earns 10 percent interest each year (about the average return of the stock market over the past 60 years). Zach decides to spend all of his extra cash.

If Aaron invests at this rate for only six years and then never puts in another dime into the account after his 28th birthday, his cash investment of $21,600 would grow to more than a million dollars by the time he was ready to retire.

If Zach wised up at age 28 and realized that he should probably start saving for retirement, he'd have to invest $300 a month for the next *35* years, or a total of $126,000, to have $1 million by age 65. Because Aaron started earlier, his smaller investment had more time to grow.

That's the power of compound interest. It can be a thing of beauty and every financial adviser will tell you that, as a young person, your best friend is time. The earlier you start compounding the better.

But very few financial advisers say anything to young people about the monumental financial benefits of starting big. Most of them fear that they'll scare you away with the "S-bomb" and the "B-word." They all believe that if they tell you "save" a large amount of your paycheck or to stick to a "budget" in order to invest in your future, you'll tune them out. Some of these guys simply believe it's impossible for you to save a large amount or invest more than a few dollars of every paycheck toward your future. This is unfortunate because investing a large amount of money early in life could add hundreds of thousands of dollars to your net worth over time. Here's a quick example to illustrate what I mean.

Let's say 22-year-old Aaron (from the example above) takes the $15K Year challenge, makes a few cutbacks and invests $8,000 into his retirement account in Year 1. Zach, on the other hand, invests $3,000. For the next 10 years, they each put $3,000 into their respective retirement accounts each year. At age 33, they stop investing—choosing instead to let their money compound independently (at an average rate of 10 percent).

At age 65, Aaron and Zach are both ready to retire. Because Aaron invested that extra $5,000 back at age 22, he will retire with close to $1.7 million, or $300,000 richer than Zach.

By starting early and starting "big" you could retire earlier or more comfortably than the average iLifer.

"But I don't *have* $8,000," you say. Chillax. Don't combust. That's what this book is for. Hopefully, that example has given you more motivation to take on the $15,000 challenge.

Yes, in order to actually pull this off, you might have to leave a couple of fierce heels at the store this year or decline a few invitations to eat out and learn how to cook. You might even have to move back in with your parents for a few months or drive a 20th century car. It will be hard at times but, remember, it's only a year and it'll be over before you know it. After a few decades, when you decide you are ready to hang up your hat and move to a beachfront property in South Florida for retirement (a decade earlier than the friends who were always inviting you out to eat, by the way), you will be happy you did it.

Now that I've got you thinking about a beachfront home in West Palm Beach, let's talk a little more about retirement.

Investing For the Future: Retirement

If you've landed a traditional full-time job, then there's a good chance that your company offers a tax-deferred 401(k) retirement program. For the purposes of this section, you don't need to know the details of this plan (there is a list of resources near the end of the chapter that will help you understand the ins and outs of retirement account options). For now, just realize that a 401(k) is the most common type of retirement nest egg fund offered by employers and that there may be free money inside.

Many employers offer a "company match" with their 401(k) system. This usually means that the company will add a percentage of your contribution up to a maximum dollar amount. For example, your employer might offer a match of 50 cents for every dollar you contribute, up to $2,500. So, in order to get the maximum match, you would need to invest $5,000 out of your paycheck, for a total investment of $7,500.

This is free money. It's such a good opportunity that most financial advisers say you should contribute enough to get the maximum company match even before you pay off your student loans or credit card debt.

> *"If your employer offers a company match on your contributions to a 401(k), your are to jump at it. Snubbing your nose at this deal is tantamount to turning down a bonus."*
>
> —SUZE ORMAN, *The Money Book for the Young, Fabulous and Broke* (2005)

But most iLifers don't take advantage of this free money opportunity. A 2006 report by Hewitt Associates, an employee benefits consulting firm, found that only 31 percent of iLifer workers (those aged 18 to 25) eligible to participate in a company 401(k) plan actually do so. This is less than half the participation rate for Gen-Xers (63 percent) and Baby Boomers (72 percent).

That's a pretty shocking statistic.

Besides a lack of awareness about the whole "free loot" aspect of the 401(k) matching system, the only rationale I can think of for this low participation rate is that most iLifers don't have enough money to contribute at the end of each month.

And it's a shame this is the case because Hewitt's report forecasts that, while the average young worker who contributes to her company 401(k) plan can expect to replace 100 percent of her preretirement income when she retires, those who don't take advantage of their 401(k) plan can only expect to replace 43 percent of their preretirement income.

THE $15,000 YEAR ENDORSES...The 401(k) Match...Free money!

I know you look forward to being a senior citizen with swagger. A genteel geriatric. A fly fogey. Unfortunately, you can't do this on 43 percent of your preretirement income. With such a small treasure chest, you'd be just getting by. No one wants to have a penny-pinching Scroogette for a great-grandmother.

Use the smart-money principles and cash-saving tips in this book to boost your savings and take full advantage of your company's free 401(k) match. Your descendants will thank you.

Below are some additional resources that will help you learn all you need to know about retirement and investing for the future. If terms like Roth IRA or portfolio diversification fly over your head or the number 59½ means absolutely nothing to you, don't worry, you're not alone. You should check out these straightforward websites and books that break down the whole issue of investing for the future. These resources will help you understand how to go about strategizing for retirement and how to allocate your funds based on your circumstances and expectations. Remember, we're on our own on this one.

WEBSITES

- www.jumpstartcoalition.org
- www.20somethingfinance.com
- www.fool.com

BOOKS

- *Get a Financial Life: Personal Finance in Your Twenties and Thirties* by Beth Kobliner (2000)
- *The Money Book for the Young, Fabulous, and Broke* by Suze Orman (2005)
- *You're So Money: Live Rich, Even When You're Not* by Farnoosh Torabi (2008)

Investing for the Future: The Stock Market

As I write, the stock market is going through one of its worst funks in recent history. In 2008, Americans experienced firsthand the vicious power of a bear market as it wiped out large fortunes overnight. It seemed that no corporation was immune. Experts were caught flat-footed as blue chips became penny stocks in a matter of months. The Dow Jones Industrial Average plunged 6,500+ points (more than 50 percent) in just 12 months and dropped to below 6,600 for the first time in 11 years on March 6, 2009.

Your folks may have lost a huge chunk of their retirement money or your childhood home may have come under the specter of foreclosure. Or you may have just grown tired of seeing front-page photos of middle-aged Wall Street traders pouting on the floor of the New York Stock Exchange.

Since most of the "experts" and Wall Street types failed epically to predict the 2008 crash, I'm going to assume you don't want to hear any more speculative advice or analysis about the stock market.

I'll keep it brief. Two points:

First, because you are young and most likely have little to lose, this is perhaps your best opportunity to invest a little more aggressively.

Let's say you have $3,200 saved in your 401(k) (the average amount for iLifers in 2006, according to Hewitt) and you want to know how to allocate it. If you put 100 percent of this money in stocks and the stock market lost 50 percent of its value, you'd be out $1,600. Losing any amount of money is rough but you'd be much better off than the average Boomer, who has $93,200 saved in his 401(k). If he were to take this aggressive all-stock approach, and the market crashed, he'd lose $46,600. That's serious dough.

Second, be warned that stock market investing is for the long-term. It should be all too clear to the 2009 or 2010 reader that the stock market is volatile and beastly when it wants to be and is not the place for short-term investments. If you will need the money in the next five years, don't put it in the stock market. Period.

For more information on how to manage your investments, please visit any of these lovely websites:

- Finance.yahoo.com
- www.morningstar.com
- moneycentral.msn.com/investor
- www.smartmoney.com/investing
- www.kiplinger.com

CLOSING NOTE ON SAVINGS, DEBT AND INVESTING FOR THE FUTURE

Taking control of your personal finances is an overarching theme of the $15,000 Year and, as a result, many of the concepts from these chapters work in tandem.

For example, the investing for the future option goes hand in hand with the idea of getting (and staying) out of debt. One final example:

Let's say you, at age 22, owe $5,000 on credit card with an interest rate of 18 percent. If you put $5,000 of your $15,000 savings towards paying that debt off immediately, you just saved yourself $900 in interest. With an 8 percent annual return rate, investing that $900 alone without ever adding a dime to it will leave you with an extra $25K by the time you're ready to retire. If you added $5,000 from your $15K savings and continued to put away a modest $50 every week for the next 10 years, you'd be a millionaire by the time you retired.

Also, the part about compound interest works in the case of savings as well. If you decide to allocate the majority of your money into an emergency fund rather than a retirement account or a collection of stocks and other investments, the power of compounding is still at work (although not as strongly). With a high-yield online account or CD, you can expect anywhere from 2 to 5 percent annual percentage yield as of May 2009. But the CDs with the best rates usually have a minimum required balance (say, $5,000). While this might be a major obstacle for most young people, the $15K-Yearer can cough up five grand, no problem.

ADDITIONAL RESOURCES

- www.youngmoney.com
- www.suzeorman.com
- www.feedthepig.com
- www.youngmoneytalks.com
- www.wesabe.com
- www.morningstar.com
- www.duedee.com (Stocks and social networking)
- www.getrichslowly.com
- www.thesimpledollar.com ("Financial talk for the rest of us.")
- www.moneychimp.com (Check out the compound interest calculator.)
- www.whatsmyscore.org ("Everything you need to know about credit.")
- www.indebtEd.com

CHAPTER 5

WORK-LIFE: iLifers and the Job Market.

"The recession provides a double whammy for the job prospects of those trying to establish themselves. There are fewer jobs to go around, and older Americans who can do so are either delaying retirement or seeking to return to the work force."

—FLOYD NORRIS FOR THE NEW YORK TIMES
YOUNGER JOB-SEEKERS HAVE IT WORSE
DECEMBER 12, 2008

iLifers, already predisposed against many of the dominant structures and cultural standards of the traditional workforce, have been faced with the additional challenge of finding and keeping jobs in the midst of economic uncertainty, massive layoffs and stiff hiring freezes. Because the recession wiped out more than $2 trillion in retirement savings, we're competing against our parents for work and, in many cases, we're losing.

While the historic 8.5 percent unemployment rate made news headlines in April 2009, most media reports did not point out that the rate was nearly 13 percent for the 20 to 29 age group. (For comparison, the unemployment rate for 20-somethings hovered around 5 percent in 1999.) Just about every economist predicted that unemployment figures would increase throughout 2009 and early 2010.

This chapter endorses the $15,000 Year as a strategy for dealing with the "double whammy" of approaching a working world that is often at odds with iLifer ideals and, at the same time, harder to get into than a pair of skinny jeans.

THE NEW OCCUPATIONAL MOBILITY

Your 20s are perhaps the most crucial years when it comes to determining which career path you will ultimately take. How you spend your Independent Life Stage will ultimately decide what career you pursue as well as how fast you make it to the top of your chosen field. Most young adults choose to take an erratic path during this time, switching jobs every couple of years (on average, Americans hold seven to eight different posts between the ages of 18 and 30).

> *"While only 10 percent of adults reported changing jobs to get a 'better job' in the recent National Compensation Survey, 27 percent of 18- to 24-year-olds and 17 percent of 25- to 34-year-olds reported doing so. This reflects the somewhat more aspirational nature of young adults as well as the fact that many have jobs that are not consistent with their career goals."*
>
> —MINTEL INTERNATIONAL, *Spending Power of Young Adults* (2008)

WORK-iLIFE BALANCE

While the pay, promotion policies and workplace culture of many entry-level jobs are often at odds with the career goals of young people, several iLifers who enter the workforce also find out that their jobs are not consistent with their *life* goals. Specifically, their social life.

The concept of "work-life balance," or the balance between your job and your personal life, has undergone a historic transformation over the last 40 years as Americans have steadily increased their working hours. Juliet Schor, author of *The Overworked American*, argues that full-time workers are now putting in 160 more hours on average each year than they did in 1969. That's equal to about an extra month of work. In the last 30 years, American workers have gone from working just slightly more hours than their European counterparts to clocking in close to 40 percent more cubicle time than French, German or Italian workers. Nearly 70 percent of Americans say they'd like to slow down or have a more relaxed life.

iLifers, who grew up amidst this trend of increased office time and saw fatigued parents come home late from work far too often, have rejected the idea that they should lead overworked and under-fulfilled lives. Because job satisfaction tends to be low among younger workers, those positions that do not offer a desirable work-life balance tend to have the highest turnover rates.

"Even though the official workweek has been pegged at 40 hours for nearly half a century, many professionals believe that they must work overtime and weekends to keep up. A 2003 national survey from the Center for a New American Dream found that 3 in 5 American feel pressure to work too much. In addition, a 2005 Conference Board study revealed that Americans are growing increasingly unhappy with their jobs."

—VICKI ROBIN AND JOE DOMINGUEZ, *Your Money or Your Life* (2008)

The $15,000 Year and the Recession: Working Through It

Below is a list of some of the most common job scenarios that iLifers have experienced as a result of the recession. (They also happen to be some of the most appropriate cases for the $15K Year.)

SCENARIO 1: You weren't able to land that corporate job with the fat salary because of a recession-induced hiring freeze. You kept applying but each time you got the same corporate sob story: "You are a highly qualified applicant and we wished we could offer you a position at our company but due to economic uncertainty…." Eventually you had the prodigal son's revelation and realized that you had parents who loved you and would accept you even if nobody else would. You decided to go home after graduation and chill for a bit before finding a local gig until things cleared up. After four tough years of schooling, you could use a break, anyways.

SCENARIO 2: The economic collapse of '08–'09 also encouraged more young people to pursue the type of service positions that they may have been reluctant to take on because of the small salary and their large student debt. Maybe you took a sharp turn from the path towards the corporate world of finance, consulting, accounting and the like and decided to go the nonprofit route. You find the work fulfilling but you don't know if you'll be able to maintain your standard of living and pay off your student loans.

SCENARIO 3: You hate your corporate desk job. It's not personally fulfilling, your talents are being underutilized and the work-life balance is a disgrace. You want to quit and take a position that is more in line with your values and vision. Sadly, in the world we live in, choosing values over big business usually means taking a pay cut. You're not sure you will be able to pay your bills if you quit.

SCENARIO 4: In the middle of your senior year (after failing to land your dream job), you had a sudden epiphany that grad school *is* for you after all. But you need to take a year off and actually apply for the next fall term. So the plan is to sign up for a one-year post or a series of internships that will pay your bills, give you an opportunity to make an immediate impact and hopefully look good on your grad school applications. Oh, and it would be nice to save up a little money so that you don't have to sleep on a futon throughout grad school.

SCENARIO 5: You were one of the lucky few who landed a corporate job but you don't see yourself staying at the company for more than two years. Your plan is to put in those 40 (or 60) weekly cubicle hours for a couple of years while being paid handsomely, then head to B-school or Med school, start your own business, or simply pursue a position in a different firm, industry or country. Your plan between now and then: enjoy the fruits of your labor (read: live the good life) and make sure you're financially stable by the time you're ready to make the switch.

SCENARIO 6: You were never a big fan of the traditional full-time workplace and you only want to work part-time while you pursue a true interest that might not make any money off the bat—fiction writing, music, film production, acting, social media, entrepreneurship, etc. You'll happily wait tables in Manhattan if it'll give you the time you need to finish your screenplay. Or you'll work as a part-time nanny so long as you have Thursdays and Fridays off to meet up with the other three members of your band to rehearse, devise marketing schemes and play the occasional Friday night dive show. But you're not sure if you'll make enough to pay your bills, replace your old electronic guitar and put in your third of the money for producing and promoting the debut album.

SCENARIO 7: You've been caught up in a sweeping round of company layoffs (along with 35 percent of the workforce). You had only been working a few months and you don't have much in the way of an emergency savings fund. You need to get by on your weekly unemployment check of $325 until you find a job. Decent positions are hard to come by and you don't know how you will get by on less than half of your pre-layoff income.

If your situation looks roughly like any of the above scenarios (or if you fear you could end up in one of the less favorable scenarios in the near future), use the savings tips in Section III to ride out the recession and seize occupational freedom at the same time.

THE $15,000 YEAR ENDORSES... Occupational Boldness... Take chances. Make mistakes. Get messy.

Pay yourself with the $15,000 you'll be saving. Wait those tables and write that screenplay. Quit that unfulfilling desk job with its comfortable salary and drab décor and go work for a women's rights organization in Uganda. Record that album or paint those portraits while you are between jobs and receiving unemployment benefits. Bide your time at that multinational company as you build up your nest egg and then surprise your coworkers by jumping off the corporate ladder to start your own business.

The government might call you underemployed. Your parents might call you a waste of tuition (don't worry they still love you and are secretly glad to have you back home). Your friends might not be able to call you because Ugandan cellular signals can be a bit patchy.

But I say you're making a bold career move during one of the only periods of your life when the risks of doing so are minimal and the costs of failing are low. And, when you're young and independent, "failure" is not really failure so long as it teaches you something and helps you direct the career course you ultimately take.

CHANGE THE WORLD.

On an individual level, the career path you choose to take and what you end up doing for a living will have a huge influence on the world you live in—whether you contribute to the greater good of society or add to the existing social problems. Additionally, the road you choose to take will definitely affect the *collective* impact that this generation has on the narrative of the 21st century.

The $15K Year gives you an the opportunity to do well *and* do good by taking on work that creates real meaning in someone else's life. You might work as a counselor that helps get inner-city students on the path towards college, or as the only medical intern at a clinic in Haiti, or as a citizen journalist who gives a voice to a neglected immigrant-community. Even if the vocational experience is only temporary, your involvement could have a permanent impact.

> *"Almost anyone—regardless of income, available time, age and skills can do something useful for others and, in the process, strengthen the fabric of our shared community."*
> —BILL CLINTON, *Giving* (2007)

And even if you aren't able to make a full-time occupational service commitment, there are plenty of other ways to contribute to society by serving on a smaller scale. You might spend one or two evenings a week helping a high school engineering team build a robot or devote one weekend a month to building houses with Habitat for Humanity or volunteer down at your church's community dinner for the homeless every third Saturday.

The chances that you will devote time to any of these service activities are reduced drastically if you're stuck putting in 60 hours a week at a job you can't stand.

Use the $15K Year to create some occupational breathing room and flexibility in your career path. Change the world by making some type of positive social impact during your time on earth. Start now.

Your children's generation will thank you.

See Appendix B for more on iLifers and the workplace.

CHAPTER 6

DREAM-FUNDING: The $15,000 Year and Entrepreneurship.

"Plenty of other laid-off workers across the country, burned out by a merciless job market, are building business plans instead of sending out résumés. For these people, recession has become the mother of invention."

—MATT RICHTEL FOR THE NEW YORK TIMES
TIRED OF LOOKING FOR WORK, SOME CREATE THEIR OWN
MARCH 13, 2009

In the world of entrepreneurship, "gerontocracy," or the idea of older people running things, has effectively been defeated during the past decade as startups founded and run by fresh-faced 20-somethings have popped up all over the country. iLifers are no longer willing to wait to bring their business ideas to fruition. It bears repeating that, for the first time in American history, 18- to 24-year-olds are starting businesses at a faster rate than 35- to 44-year-olds. According to the 2007 "Open Ages" survey of entrepreneurs by American Express, we are also three times more likely than young Baby Boomers to start our own businesses right out of college. We are twice as likely as Baby Boomers to plan to be "serial" entrepreneurs, owning more than one business. Seventy percent of today's high schoolers plan on owning their own businesses, a recent Gallup poll found (yes, that's the most ever too). Half of all 2009 college graduates believe that self-employment is more secure than a full-time job.

There are a bunch of social, demographic, cultural and economic factors that might explain why young people are hitting the startup circuit in numbers previously seen as unimaginable. We're the first generational cohort to grow up in a world where young, brazen business owners have been constantly featured and glorified in popular culture. While Boomers may have felt that actors or athletes had the most glamorous and enjoyable jobs, iLifers rank entrepreneurs like Facebook founder Mark Zuckerburg near the top of that list as well. Another proposed explanation is that we are simply less patient and more self-important than previous youths. We grew up hearing that our thoughts and ideas were special and now we are taking that mindset to the business world. There's also the argument that iLifers don't mesh well with the stiff structural and cultural landscape of the traditional workplace and would rather have the flexibility and autonomy of being self-employed.

While these and other theories are all likely factors, let's take a look at two other factors that relate to the $15K Year: "We Can" and "We Care."

We Can

> *"I know I can… be what I want to be."*
> —NAS, *I Can* (circa 2002)

When it comes to entrepreneurship, the advancement of technology has completely changed the game. Because of the low start-up costs and scalability of the Web, most of the barriers that have historically prevented young people from branching out on their own have been eliminated.

THE "HOW TO" MOVEMENT: WE KNOW "HOW TO" (OR CAN EASILY FIND OUT)

Eighty percent of universities now have courses in entrepreneurship, most of which teach students how to harness the power of technology to formulate, launch and sustain a business venture. There are hundreds of free tutorials online that provide step-by-step guidance for how to do basically anything one can imagine. From creation to promotion to distribution, it is possible to handle a growing number of projects in-house without relying on experts. After watching a few 10-minute video tutorials on Youtube and reading a few online forums, you might learn the basics of what you need to know to create a short film with Final Cut Pro and embed it on your website (or pitch it to a major studio). The Internet has unleashed thousands of new forms of creative expression and each new phenomenon is usually accompanied by dozens of tutorials about how to DIY.

DIY

"Although he had years of programming experience, [Ethan] Nicholas, who is 30, had never built a game in Objective-C, the coding language of the iPhone. So he searched the Internet for tips and informal guides, and used them to figure out the iPhone software development kit that Apple puts out.

Because he grew up playing shoot-em-up computer games, he decided to write an artillery game. He sketched out some graphics and bought inexpensive stock photos and audio files.

For six weeks, he worked 'morning, noon and night'— by day at his job on the Java development team at Sun, and after-hours on his side project....

After the project was finished, Mr. Nicholas sent it to Apple for approval, quickly granted, and iShoot was released into the online Apple store on Oct. 19.

When he checked his account with Apple to see how many copies the game had sold, Mr. Nicholas's jaw dropped: On its first day, iShoot sold enough copies at $4.99 each to net him $1,000. He and (his wife) Nicole were practically 'dancing in the street,' he said.

The second day, his portion of the day's sales was about $2,000."

JENNA WORTHAM for The New York Times
THE IPHONE GOLD RUSH
April 3, 2009

MOVE IT, GATEKEEPERS!

The traditional business models of industries such as music, film production, and publishing have all been transformed by technological advances that have effectively reduced the role of middlemen, who traditionally stood between the public and artists, writers and innovators. It's never been easier or cheaper to create, promote and distribute an album, book or short film.

The same goes for new media ventures such as social web. As you read this, there are hundreds of Web 2.0 enterprises being created by pajama-ed 21-year-olds in dorm rooms and bare apartments across the country. Today's young inventors can launch innovative, scalable ventures to a global audience without tons of capital and without any permission from the powers that be. In the uncharted terrain of the Wild, Wild Web, there are few powerbrokers that have the ability to determine which products will succeed. In most cases, whether or not a venture goes viral and subsequently global depends on the kind of buzz it garners through "word of mouse."

WE ARE FREE TO TAKE RISKS

Depending on what statistics you believe, somewhere between 40 and 70 percent of new businesses fail or fail to make any money in the first couple of years of operation. Relative to older Americans, iLifers find this high failure rate less daunting because we have much less riding on our success. Most iLifers have little to lose and are free of the type of financial and familial obligations that often make the risks involved in entrepreneurship prohibitive. And most of us realize that this is the only time in our adult lives when we will know such freedom. The "Open Ages" survey found that nearly three quarters of iLifer entrepreneurs (72 percent) say they "like to take risks" compared to just over half of Baby Boomers (53 percent).

We Care

Despite the glitz and media hype that have surrounded a few of the young entrepreneurs who have excelled in the software, gadget and social media worlds, the vast majority of 20-somethings who take the entrepreneurial route do so for reasons other than money. According to a 2007 report by *Young Money* magazine, only 15 percent of iLifers who start businesses are driven by higher earnings potential*.

The same data show that 55 percent of young people get involved in entrepreneurship because they are passionate about an idea or an issue. Many of us believe we can have a positive impact on society through our ventures. We've grown up seeing images of genocide, poverty and injustice in distant locales and in our local communities throughout the crises-stricken 1990s and 2000s. This has sparked a rise in social entrepreneurship, or the idea of starting nonprofit organizations or business ventures that are designed to address systemic problems and have a positive impact on society.

One example is a magazine called *Good,* which is dedicated to the idea of social entrepreneurship. It was launched by 26-year-old Max Schorr in 2007 and has a pay-what-you-want subscription business

*Supporting this finding, the American Express study found that only 18 percent of young startup starters are interested in money.

model, with 100 percent of the proceeds going to benefit a non-profit of the consumer's choice*.

Dreams Deferred

Even though 50 percent of young people list starting their own business as a goal, labor statistics show that less than 5 percent have actually done so. Even with cost-reducing digital technology, the elimination of traditional gatekeepers and the freedom to take risks, most young people simply don't have enough capital to fund their business ventures. Many are toiling for too many hours in the corporate workforce to be able to dedicate any serious time or energy to entrepreneurship and don't have enough saved up to leave their jobs and pursue their dreams.

> *"Sixty percent of [iLifers] name lack of capital as the main reason they cannot engage in entrepreneurship."*
> —YOUNG MONEY MAGAZINE, *Legacy in the Making* (2007)

This is why entrepreneurship is probably the most dynamic of all possible motivations for undertaking the $15,000 Year. By reducing consumer expenditures by $15K, you can set yourself up for entrepreneurial success. Use the $15,000† or some portion of it as the initial investment in an entrepreneurial venture that you think will make a little money or have a major positive impact. Or both.

> *"Don't let your dreams be dreams..."*
> —JACK JOHNSON, *Dreams Be Dreams* (circa 2003)

PERSONAL NOTE: This is the most personal of the options for me as the book you hold in your hands is a result of a consumption slowdown. I'd do it over again in a heartbeat and I probably will.

There's no $15,000 prize package of smartphones, restaurant meals, flatscreens, sneakers, concerts or nice furniture that I would

---

*www.goodmagazine.com

†Although $15,000 is more than enough to get many types of businesses and ventures off the ground, in some cases, $15,000 won't be sufficient to completely cover the start up costs of your project (e.g., major social media projects). But, not to worry. You can also use the money to support yourself while you drop out of the traditional workforce to develop the business model and solicit venture capitalists for the necessary funds. Ask any successful Silicon Valley entrepreneur and they'll tell you that finding investors to fund their innovative ideas can be a full-time job in itself.

accept in place of the experiences I've had starting my own publishing company and writing a book on a topic that I feel strongly about. Don't get me wrong. Like any entrepreneurial venture it required a ton of hard work—but it has opened up a ton of doors for me and it's an experience that I'll have for the rest my life. I love gadgets as much as the next guy, but my cell phones only last for about two years, assuming I don't drop them in a pool of liquid or on a hard surface before I'm eligible for an upgrade.

See the Afterword for the behind-the-scenes-story of this book.

BONUS CHAPTER!

7 More Reasons...

Still debating? Here are a few more reasons to cut back, ride out the recession, and change the world.

1. **GO GREEN, LIVE RICH.** One of the side effects of reducing consumption is that you automatically reduce your ecological footprint. Between 1970 and 2004 (as consumerism intensified), greenhouse gases from humans rose 70 percent. The UN Convention on Climate Change recently made it very clear that we cannot continue with this unsustainable practice of consuming the earth's scarce resources at such a fast pace. There will be plenty of tips in the next section that will help you save money and save the planet at the same time. You'll learn how to cut your expenditures on utilities (Chapter 8), transportation (Chapter 9) and apparel (Chapter 12) while simultaneously taking part in the green movement.

2. **ACTS 20:35b* (GIVING).** Donate a portion of your savings charitably. Give money to strangers on the street or to established foundations. The poor and those who fight for the poor were hit especially hard by the recession as charitable contributions dried up. Go against the grain. Find qualified charities at www.GuideStar.org or www.charitywatch.org.

---

*"*And remember the words of the Lord Jesus, that He said, 'It is more blessed to give than to receive.'*" (New King James Version)

3. **LOSE WEIGHT, LIVE HEALTHY.** The childhood obesity rate has tripled during the past three decades and some of the largest increases occurred during the 1990s, when iLifers were in elementary and middle schools. As you work to reduce consumer expenditures, you can simultaneously reduce your consumption of expensive and fatty fast food and eat more healthily. For example, drinking water exclusively for a year could save you $600+ and you'd have less trouble shedding those extra inches. See Chapter 10 on food for more information.

4. **FIRST GENERATION OF "GLOBAL CITIZENS."** If you, like many iLifers who have grown up in a digitally connected world, consider yourself to be a global citizen, the $15,000 Year is a way to show just how committed you are to this concept. While it may feel like a huge sacrifice to reduce expenditures down to $20,000 for the year, at least 80 percent of humanity lives on less than $10 per day ($3,650 per year). Forcing yourself to go without certain things will give you a small, partial idea of how most of our global neighbors live on a daily basis. There's a good chance that this will make you more compassionate (and generous) towards the problem of global poverty as you move forward in your life.

   For example, one of the tips you will find in Chapter 10 on "Food" is the "monthly fast." You set aside one day each month and eat nothing before sundown. The point of doing this is not only to help you save $88 over the course of the year, but, more importantly, to give you a deeper understanding of what many of our global peers face not once a month, but every day. Hunger continues to affect billions of lives each year even as Americans throw away 25 percent of the food they buy—enough to feed all of the world's underfed population. If you are bold enough to try out this fast, the intense hunger pangs you feel starting around noon and returning intermittently throughout the day will create a bond between you and two-thirds of the world's population (i.e., those who are either underfed or starving). The intense joy you feel as you tear into a hot dinner (and realize that you never knew Easy Mac could taste so good) will hopefully encourage you to put a similar smile on the face of a slumdog orphan in Bangalore by donating to an NGO, supporting your church's mission trip or emailing your Congresswoman and asking her to fight for increased global development aid in the next spending bill.

5. **BOYCOTT CONSUMERISM.** Black Friday 2008, turned out to truly be a dark day in the history of America's consumption-driven society. At a Wal-Mart in Long Island, Jdimytai Damour, a temp worker, was trampled to death by a mob of sale-crazed shoppers as the store opened its doors. Four other people, including a pregnant woman, were also injured. The savagery that took place in Long Island and at shopping centers around the country exposed the extent to which our social order has prioritized things over human life. Take this year to distance yourself from consumerism and you'll probably realize that you can actually live a full and happy life without falling into the work-and-spend cycle that has dominated society.

> *"Jdimytai Damour died because too many of us have bought, heart and soul, into the great lie of American consumerism: acquiring stuff will make you whole."*
>
> —Leonard Pitts for the Miami Herald, *Our Destructive Love of Stuff*, December 3, 2008

6. **CONSUMER POWER.** Become a more informed consumer and make the most out of every purchase—never again spend money on a subpar product or service or pay full price for an online purchase when there is a 20-percent-off coupon code floating around in cyberspace for the taking. This is a skill that you will keep for the rest of your life. Use this year to learn the fundamental art of dollar-stretching.

7. **GANDHI DID IT.** When Mahatma Gandhi was a young student in England, he engaged in the 19th century version of the $15,000 Year. In his autobiography, he recounts making the decision to cut his expenditures by half, keep a record of all his spending and bring his financial habits in line with his values in his early 20s. And, he recalls, he had a great time doing it.

> *"Let not the reader think that this living made my life by any means a dreary affair. On the contrary the change harmonized my inward and outward life. It was also more in keeping with the means of my family. My life was certainly more truthful and my soul knew no bounds of joy."*
>
> —Mahatma Gandhi, *An Autobiography: The Story of My Experiments with Truth* (1929)

What better way to make an impact than to follow in the footsteps of Gandhi, who coined the phrase "Be the change you want to see in the world?"

III.

CHAPTER 7

THE SETUP.

So you've decided to give this $15,000 Year thing a try and cut back on your expenditures for 12 months in order to gain some financial security, embrace occupational boldness and/or change the world. Great. You've come to the right section. The ensuing pages are full of advice that will help you reach your savings goal without cramping your lifestyle. You'll learn how to pick a budget-friendly apartment, how to go car-free or car-lite, how to cook a meal for less than a dollar, how to embrace frugal fashion and a bunch of other "how-tos."

But, before we get into the good stuff, we need to handle some administrative business and get you set up. I'll try to make this as quick and painless as possible.

STATISTICALLY SPEAKING

The 2007 Consumer Expenditure Survey (CES) by the U.S. Bureau of Labor Statistics (BLS) features heavily in this section—it's the source of most of the spending calculations and price information you will see. The CES, a nationwide household survey designed to find out how Americans spend their money, is the most detailed account of consumer purchasing patterns and expenditure information. Because this survey tracks spending patterns by age groups, it works perfectly for iLifers who want to know exactly where to cut back in order to meet their savings target.

HOW THE $15K SAVINGS WILL BE CALCULATED

Based primarily on the "under-25" age group data from the CES, average salary statistics for recent college graduates, the national savings rate and various forms of market research, each chapter will offer information about current spending patterns for the average iLifer as well as suggested spending targets that would lead the *average* young consumer to $15,000 savings. Since these stats and recommendations are tailored to our standard iLifer, "Stan D'ard" (Salary: **$35,000 after taxes**), you may need to adjust your spending targets to suit your individual situation* (See box below).

OUR STANDARD ILIFER

Name: Stan D'ard
Age: 22.5
Occupation: Marketing analyst
Salary: $35,000 (after taxes)
Pre-15K-Year Savings Rate: 3 percent
Pre-$15K-Year Savings: $856
Credit Card Debt: $1,084
Student Loans: $19,007
Average 401(k) contribution: $0 per month

TARGET SPENDING BUDGET FOR $15,000 YEAR

ANNUAL: $20,000
MONTHLY: $1,667

Here's a quick rundown of what you'll see in the next five chapters (each chapter focuses on one of the five major areas of spending specified by the CES):

- Chapter 8: Housing
- Chapter 9: Transportation
- Chapter 10: Food
- Chapter 11: Entertainment
- Chapter 12: Apparel & Appearance

These five categories account for more than 90 percent of the out-of-pocket consumer expenditures of the under-25 consumer (excluding education-related costs). You'll see more than $50,000 worth of saving options and each tip comes with a calculated estimate of "ANNUAL SAVINGS," giving you a finish-line view of the payoffs that can result from making minor changes over the course of a year.

---

*If you don't yet have a steady income, you can set your target spending budget at $15,000 for the year ($1,250 per month).

STEP ONE: EMAIL ACTION PLAN

Using the Internet to save money is one of the recurring themes you will see in the following chapters and this is one of the ways this book differs from your average budget guide.

You'll find info about dozens of websites that may help you save hundreds, if not thousands on your yearly expenses. But, you know the drill: no free lunch. Many of these sites will ask you to register and cough up your email address so that they can send you promotional mail—some of which will be useful, some of which will be spam.

To make things easier for you, one of the first things you need to do is establish an email action plan that will allow you to save money without having to worry about a bunch of promotional fluff getting mixed in together with the important stuff in your inbox. You may already have a system for filtering such messages but, if not, the $15,000 Year endorses a three-pronged email strategy that will help you manage the onslaught of propaganda that comes with the territory of Web 2.0 frugality:

PRIMARY ACCOUNT: This is the account you already have and use daily. You get your bank alerts here as well as your airline travel confirmations. You probably chat with this account or use it to send inappropriate Youtube clips to your friends from your cubicle (corporate email accounts are usually bugged).

Who Gets It? Only your most trusted, revered and dependable retailers and online communities. Guard this address like you would your phone number. Only give it to those merchants who will respect it enough not to bombard your inbox every other day with spam messages.

SECONDARY ACCOUNT: You may or may not already have such an account. This is the email address you check twice a week at most.

Who Gets It? Give this email address to online retailers and savings websites that might have a good sale or money tip every once in a while. You can also give this address out in person when you attend a free event and there's a mailing list signup sheet. Check back here every now and again to see if there's anything worth following up on.

TERTIARY ACCOUNT: This is the account you use for those pesky websites that make you register and receive a "confirmation" email before you can access their content. If you run into one of these sites and you don't expect you will have any use for their weekly emails in the future, give them this email account, get your access, and then forget about them. This is also the default address for any site that doesn't make the cut for the first two addresses but may occasionally provide useable emails. Check this account a couple times a month when you're bored.

> NOTE: If you have trouble keeping track of all your passwords, look up a safe password storage program that will save your login information for you (or just save them yourself in your cell phone and on your laptop's hard drive).

YOU CAN'T SPEND WHAT YOU CAN'T SEE

If you've decided to have a certain amount saved in an emergency fund or a 401(k) account by the end of the $15K Year, set up a direct deposit that will automatically siphon a portion of your paycheck into the appropriate account. Once you don't have the money at your disposal, you'll be surprised by how easy it is to live without it... especially with this book in hand.

> NOTE: You can also make an arrangement with your bank to have your entire credit card balance paid off out of your checking account each month so that you don't have to pay any interest.

THE BOLD.

While most of the $15K Year tips in this section allow you to save money and save face, in order to pull this off, you may have to be a little bold at times and push the limits of your comfort zone. Don't worry—a little embarrassment never hurt anybody. Remember, your bank account will be better for it.

BOLD IS...

- Asking a friend of a friend to let you couch surf for a couple nights during your apartment-searching trip in a new city. [*SAVINGS*: ***$217***]
- Speaking up when you're out at dinner and your friends try to "split the check." (Everyone else ordered expensive drinks and you had a glass of water.) [*SAVINGS*: ***$8***]
- Stopping by Goodwill to buy furniture, books or clothes. [*SAVINGS*: ***$270***]
- Asking the cashier at Goodwill for a discount. [*SAVINGS*: ***$26***]
- Making a U-Turn and putting that curbed office chair into your backseat. [*SAVINGS*: ***$48***]
- Returning a sweater you bought after 27 days because you came in $31 over budget for the month (See "Keeping Records"). [*SAVINGS*: ***$34.99***]

Keeping Records

In order to successfully complete the $15,000 Year, you'll need to keep a record of your out-of-pocket spending. There are two potential ways to do this: "new school" and "old school." While I hardly ever side with old-fashioned systems when there are 21st century alternatives, my endorsement goes to the traditional method on this one. I'll introduce the new school option and then explain why I think the age-old approach is more appropriate for the $15K-Yearer. Of course, the final choice is yours but **THIS IS THE MOST IMPORTANT STEP YOU WILL TAKE TOWARDS PULLING THIS THING OFF**. I can't emphasize this enough: Keeping track of every dollar you spend will not only help you calculate your $15,000 savings—it will also fundamentally change the way you think about money.

NEW SCHOOL: MINT.COM

Mint.com is a relatively new personal finance service that prides itself in being unlike any of its predecessors. Created by an iLifer*, it provides an intuitive, easy-to-use platform for financial management, offering email reminders, savings tips and debt repayment strategies—all handled digitally on your computer (or iPhone). It's extremely user-friendly, it updates automatically and, most importantly, it's free to use.

> *"Mint.com is an online personal finance tool that tells you exactly how you're spending your money, how you can save, when your credit card payment is due, and when your bank balance is low. Sounds like mom, but without the nagging. Mint.com now has 600,000 registered users and half of them are under age 30."*
>
> —DONNA FENN for Inc. magazine, *The Entrepreneurial Generation*, December 10, 2008

Mint works well for the $15,000 Year participant because it allows you to set your target budget in major spending areas (e.g., groceries, entertainment) and chart your finances to see whether or not you are over or under budget for the month. It will help you categorize your debt and pay it down wisely or build up an emergency fund with a recommended bank.

---

*Aaron Patzer started Mint at the age of 25. After spending two years at a software startup, he had built up about $100,000 in savings and decided to quit his job and pursue entrepreneurship. He holed himself up in his room for months crafting the alpha version of Mint and the rest is history. The site was named one of the top 50 websites of 2008 by Time magazine.

OLD SCHOOL: THE BUDGET DIARY

If you decide not to use Mint (or any other online financial planner), this book endorses a tried and true and thoroughly 20th century stand-by: the physical budget diary. Most financial advisers are afraid to tell young people to use one of these, and I can understand why. Nothing sounds more middle-aged or 1980ish than a budget diary. But they work. Try it out for a month and you'll immediately notice changes in your spending habits.

HOW TO KEEP A BUDGET DIARY: $15K-YEAR STYLE

Get a large three-ring binder (at least two inches at the spine) and 11 dividers.

To start off, fill it with about 30 pages of loose-leaf paper. On the front of each page, write the appropriate day and date, starting with the first of the month on page 1 (e.g., Wednesday, July 1).

Every time you make a consumer purchase (e.g., groceries, car repair, clothes), save the receipt in your wallet or wherever you keep your debit card, driver's license and other important plastics. At the end of each day (or every other day) staple the receipts on the page of the appropriate date and jot down a quick note saying:

1. What category the expense/purchase falls under (e.g., a gas purchase counts as "Transportation" spending and a grocery trip falls under "Food" expenditures) and;
2. How much the total costs were.

Since eating is a daily activity (and one that can eat up a huge portion of your budget if not monitored carefully), there should be a daily entry under the "Food" heading, where you record what you had for breakfast, lunch and dinner and how much each of these meals cost you. If you cooked a meal, the total cost would be $0 (since you paid for the ingredients during earlier groceries trips and have accounted for them on previous days). Add up the costs of these three meals (plus whatever groceries you bought) and put a circle around the total (you will use it later).

> NOTE: This is also a good way to monitor your eating habits and move towards a healthier diet.

At the bottom of every page, write **TCE** for "Total Consumer Expenditures" and, after adding up all the expenses from that day, place the total next to TCE and put a circle around it (See Example 1).

EXAMPLE 1

Friday, March 13, 2009

Food

Breakfast: *Cooked*: Eggs and cheese quesadilla – **$0**
Lunch: *Takeout*: Treehouse Eatery—Steak plate – **$8.66**
Dinner: *Leftovers*: Steak leftovers from Treehouse – **$0**

Groceries: A gallon of milk (on sale) and 2-for-1 ground beef – **$6.11**

TOTAL FOOD: $14.77

Transportation

Gas: Refilled tank – **$16.83**

TCE: $31.60

Receipt:
ABC GROCERY STORE
WE SELL FOR LESS

1GALMLK........................$2.33
1GRDBF..........................$3.78
1GRDBF..........................$3.78
COUPON...................$3.78 –
TOTAL..............................$6.11
AMTSAVED..............$3.78
3/13/09 5:55 PM

Receipt:
SANTA CLARA SHELLRON

3/13/09 6:14:09

Pump#4
7.018 G @ $ 2.399
Unlead/Self $16.83
TOTAL **$16.83**

THANK YOU FOR CHOOSING SHELLRON

Receipt:
THE TREEHOUSE
THANK YOU. COME AGAIN.
3/13/2009
#0125 2:52PM

STEAK RANCH PLT $8.00
TAX1..................................$0.66
TO GO
TOTAL................................**$8.66**

On the 15th of every month, you are to do two very important things:

First, list your fixed monthly expenses such as rent, car payment, insurance*, most recent cell phone bill and utilities bill. Add up your fixed monthly expenses and write down the total under the heading "**Fixed Monthly Total**," (or FMT). Then compute your TCE for that day. Your TCE for the 15th of each month will be the total of your regular out-of-pocket expenditures on that day as well as all your monthly bills. It will be much higher than your other TCEs—for example, it may total $1,092 ($1,055 for monthly rent, utilities, car payment, cell phone and insurance and $37 for the food and gas you bought on that particular day).

---

*If you have expenses that you pay less frequently than once a month, such as insurance, calculate your yearly total, divide by 12 and add this number to your fixed monthly expenses list.

Once you've done this, it's time for your **Half-Month Checkup**. There are different options for how detailed you want to get when you do this but I'll just give you the basics:

On a blank page that has not been allocated to any specific date, write "Half-Month Checkup" at the top. With a calculator in hand and the scrutinizing eye of a politician looking for pork in a spending bill, flip through the first 15 days of the month and review your expenditures. Add up all of the TCEs at the bottom of each page and compute the total on the Half-Month Checkup page. This is how much you have spent so far in the month. (Feel free to go into further detail and separate your totals for food, entertainment, transportation, apparel and other major expense categories. See Example 2.)

EXAMPLE 2

HALF MONTH CHECKUP: AUGUST

Fixed Monthly Bills..*$1,055.41*

Out-of-Pocket Expenditures...............................*$322.94*

Food *$113.15*
Transportation (Gas).........*$90.17*
Entertainment...............*$50.79*
Apparel...........................*$41.50*
Other................................*$27.33*

TOTAL OUT-OF-POCKET EXPENDITURES: $1,378.35

This is a crucial step that is designed to help you examine your consumer habits, recalibrate your spending and make whatever lifestyle changes necessary in order to finish each month on budget.

If you've set a total monthly expenditures target of $1,725 and you've spent $1,378 at the halfway mark on fixed monthly expenditures and on daily out-of-pocket outlays, then you know that you can only spend $347 in the remaining two weeks of the month in order to stay under your target. With that in the back of your mind (and with all of your major monthly expenditures accounted for), you'll have increased motivation to control your day-to-day spending.

If you are on budget at the halfway point, great. Tread carefully during the rest of the month and try your best to stay within the limits you've set for yourself. If you find that you've spent too much in the first 15 days, put your recession game face on. This is your chance to make a bold, do-or-die decision about how you will proceed through the rest of the month. Decide where you need to cut back, what you need to postpone, and how you will live on the amount left over for the month. If necessary, impose a two-week moratorium on all discretionary spending—only put out money for absolute essentials.

At the end of the month, add up all of your TCEs and write down your total consumer expenditures for the month. If you were able to stay within your target budget, feel good about being that much closer to $15,000 in savings. If you were under budget, take that extra money and do something nice for yourself (go back to that store where you left the dress on the rack and buy it with pride rather than with credit). Or invest the money in one of your $15,000 Year projects—put a little more cash into your 401(k), open a business account for your entrepreneurial venture or give a little more to your church or a service foundation.

If you came in over budget, don't be discouraged, but do step your game up. Page through your binder and look back over your purchases critically. Think about which expenditures were avoidable, where you could have showed more restraint, when you could have declined temptations or peer pressure to spend, and which purchases were simply not worth the money in hindsight*. Make a commitment to come in under budget the next month and get yourself back on track.

> NOTE: If you make non-consumer expenditures (e.g., you give an offering at church, buy a software program for your entrepreneurial project, or pay $250 towards your student loan), you are welcome to write these in your budget diary as well. But make sure you don't include these when you compute your TCE totals. The $15K Year is about reducing out-of-pocket consumer expenditures, not slowing down charitable contributions or debt-repayment.

---

*One of the benefits of keeping a physical binder (rather than a digital account) is that you have receipts of everything you have purchased. By keeping all your receipts, you'll be able to return whatever items you haven't used if you find yourself over budget.

DEBIT CARDS

This book encourages the use of a debit card for the majority of purchases. Most budgeting books cite psychoanalytical findings showing that people spend more money when they use plastic than when they pay with cold hard cash. This is true. But, I think you are a smart person and you can consciously control your spending without trying to psycho-strategize against yourself.

Two reasons debit cards are the best payment option for the $15,000 Year:

1. You'll have an online record of all the purchases you make. This is great for helping you review how you spend your money*.
2. Debit cards offer the convenience of plastic without the danger of credit cards. Not only are credit cards the worst form of payment when it comes to the psychological likeliness to splurge, they also can cause you to pay even more than what's on the receipt if you either forget to pay your bill on time or carry over a balance and take on interest charges on top of what you owe. Try to use your credit card only when you are certain you can pay off the balance at the end of the month.

I understand that the old school budget diary idea might be a bit of a turnoff but it's crucial—after the year is over, feel free to burn your budget book and never think about it again (although, you'd be surprised at how paging through a yearlong spending record is sort of like reading a chapter of your autobiography).

A physical item that you keep in a prominent place is harder to neglect or forget about than a digital account. Having a binder with a record of all your expenditures will also help you come tax time, especially if your tax situation is complex. If your business gets audited in the future, you'll have receipts to verify your expenditures.

THE $15,000 YEAR ENDORSES... The Budget Diary.

Keeping a yearlong budget diary could be the difference between the person who starts the $15,000 Year but quits after a month and the person who makes it to the finish line, debt-free and financially secure.

* Use online banking as a backup if you slip up and forget to record some of your purchases on a given day.

NOTE: It may be helpful for you to take a practice month to adjust to this setup. Spend the first few weeks studying your spending and chronicling what changes you will need to make in order to meet your savings goals in various areas of your budget.

GANDHI ENDORSES... The Budget Diary

"I kept account of every farthing I spent, and my expenses were carefully calculated. Every little item such as omnibus fares or postage or a couple of coppers spent on newspapers, would be entered, and the balance struck every evening before going to bed. That habit has stayed with me ever since, and I know that as a result, though I have had to handle public funds amounting to lakhs, I have succeeded in exercising strict economy in their disbursement, and instead of outstanding debts have had invariably a surplus balance in respect of all the movements I have led. Let every youth take a leaf out of my book and make it a point to account for everything that comes into and goes out of his pocket, and like me he is sure to be a gainer in the end."

—MAHATMA GANDHI, *An Autobiography: The Story of My Experiments with Truth* (1929)

NEW SCHOOL TWIST!
Go to www.iLifers.com to download a free copy of the Budget Diary template, which you can customize and print out.

CHAPTER 8

HOUSING.

"The prettiest thing, I ever did see,
Was dusty as the handle on the door,
Rusty as a nail stuck in the old pine floor,
Looks like Home to me."

—NORAH JONES, *THE PRETTIEST THING* (circa 2004)

SPENDING BREAKDOWN

iLIFER: STAN D'ARD

CURRENT: Pre-$15,000-Year Expenditures
ANNUAL: $11,033*
MONTHLY: $919

TARGET: $15,000 Year Expenditures (**LIVING AT HOME**)
ANNUAL: $660
MONTHLY: $55

TARGET: $15,000 Year Expenditures (**LIVING ON HIS OWN**)
ANNUAL: $6,120
MONTHLY: $510

SAVINGS: **$4,913–$10,373**

Going after the big fish is one of the top strategies for pulling off the $15K Year and, when it comes to major expenditures, housing is the granddaddy of them all. It's the single largest expense you will have this year and, naturally, there are a ton of ways to dissect it for savings opportunities. This section covers a few of them and offers thousands of dollars worth of savings advice. Here's a breakdown of what you'll see in the following pages.

- A Case for Living at Home
- On Your Own (On Location)
- Finding the Perfect Apartment at the Right Price
- Furnishing Your Crib
- Saving on Utilities

*Includes rent, utilities, furniture, appliances, housekeeping supplies and household services.

A Case for Living At Home

Imagine your boss offers you a $12,000 raise, with no strings attached—no extra hours, no working weekends, no additional responsibilities. The only stipulation is that you have to live with your parents for a year. Do you take it?

Even before the economic recession, a growing number of recent grads were deciding to give themselves this de facto pay raise by living with their parents for a temporary period after graduation. Depending on which statistics you trust, somewhere between 40 and 60 percent of graduates move home after college. With a tanking economy and the need for financial security more crucial than ever, the $15K Year fully endorses this temporary repatriation. Here's why:

This is by far the easiest way to get on the path to $15K savings. Not only do you potentially save more than $8,000 in rent payments, but you also stand to save thousands in other areas.

WHAT *ELSE* YOU MIGHT SAVE BY LIVING AT HOME

- Free Utilities: ***$1,079***
- Free Food: ***$2,382*** (assuming you cut your food bill in half)
- Free Cable: ***$708***
- Free Laundry: ***$107***
- No security deposit: ***$575***

TOTAL: ***$4,851***

That's the first "pro" of living at home—infectious savings that will put you on the super fast track to $15,000 (or more) in pocketed money. If you are able to do this, you may not even need to cut back in some of the other areas described in the chapters ahead to make the $15K cut (although it wouldn't hurt to save a little extra cash).

The second motivation for a post-college homecoming has to do with the unattractiveness of alternative: renting. Since, according to federal statistics, 84 percent of under-25 independents are renters, there's a good chance that if you don't plan on living at home, you'll be renting.

While almost all Americans rent for some period in their lives—and the nomadic 20s tend to be the most appropriate time to do so—there are a few financial drawbacks associated with renting an apartment right out of school. First of all, getting your foot into the apartment door is an incredibly expensive and traditionally stressful process for the young or first-time renter. You need to have at least a couple thousand bucks saved up to cover the upfront (and hidden) costs of moving into your own place and you often need to undergo a credit check, provide references and have proof of steady income. For the recent grad who is adjusting to a new job, handling student loan repayment, and dealing with taxes and retirement investments for the first time, all of this "real world" stuff can be a more than a little overwhelming. This is one of the reasons so many people who rush into apartment life make major mistakes and end up having to move back home.

Across the age spectrum, Americans spend about 33 cents of every dollar earned on housing. A 2008 report by BLS senior economist Geoffrey Paulin revealed that today's young, unmarried adults are spending a much larger share of their incomes on housing than their counterparts 25 years ago. In 1984, housing made up 23.7 percent of the out-of-pocket expenditures made by single people age 21 to 29. By 2007, this number had jumped to 32.5 percent.

NOTE: When you rent, you are spending the largest portion of your paycheck on an item that will always belong to someone else. Unlike homeowners, renters don't gain equity, don't reap tax advantages and usually can't personalize their space (e.g., painting, remodeling) or set their own lifestyle rules (e.g., volume preferences, pets).

THE $15,000 YEAR ENDORSES... Ditching the Rent and Living With The 'Rents...

If possible, spend this year (or some portion of it) living at home and building up the kind of five-figure savings that will allow you to:

1. Save enough upfront cash to move into a decent apartment.
2. Establish a Down Payment Fund that will accelerate your path to homeownership.
3. Build up the type of credit profile and work history that will get you into the apartment of your choice, no problem (and get you a better home loan down the road).
4. Ease your introduction into the world of adulthood, rather than cramming all of your major life changes and difficult decisions into the three-month post-graduation period.

Finally, I truly believe it's never been easier to deal with the actual day-to-day reality of being a young adult living with your parents. Let's break this down in a few different ways:

Moving Back is the New Black. As post-graduation repatriation has grown more popular in recent years—AARP reports a 25 percent increase in multigenerational households since 2000—the social stigma associated with living with one's parents has all but evaporated. There are a number of reasons for this, but my favorite is based on another statistic from economist Geoffrey Paulin's comparative research: Since 1985, the percentage of single, 20-something homeowners has doubled. A growing number of grads are heading back home so that they can become homeowners in their mid-20s instead of waiting until mid-life. When people hear your rationale for living with your folks, they're more likely to say, "Why didn't I think of that?" than to laugh behind your back.

We Need Some Space. The size of the average American home grew from 983 square feet in 1950 to 2,434 square feet in 2005, making privacy less of an issue for repatriating grads than it has been in the past. With younger siblings more likely to be off to college due to the rise in educational attainment, many of today's grads are claiming up to 800 or 900 square feet of personal living space inside their childhood homes. That's probably more than what you'll get in your first apartment and the rent is minimal or nonexistent.

Parental Control. iLifers, as we saw in the Prologue, are the most *wanted* generation. Our parents are often happy to have us back. Additionally, generational scholars have consistently found that today's 20-somethings tend to have much healthier relationships with their parents relative to previous cohorts of young Americans. You may or may not think this applies to your situation but, according to the research, you are much better off than Gen-Xers when it comes to parental control. Although having to submit one's autonomy, standards of cleanliness and freedom of movement to parental jurisdiction might be a tough pill for the young homecomer, today's iLifers have it much better than their predecessors.

Hopefully, what you just read has convinced those of you who have landed a job in your hometown (or in any town with a relative) as well as those who are still looking for a job to make a one-year commitment to your future by living at "Home." Next step: convincing your folks to let you have your old room back and, possibly more challenging, convincing them to let you stay for free.

> *"Home is the place where, when you have to go there, they have to take you in."*
>
> —Robert Frost

The iLifer's Guide to Scoring a Rent-Free Year at Home

"Give me one reason to pay here..."

Sit your guardians down and ask them to give you a good reason for why they now expect rent for you living at home—after all, they never asked for any the first 18 years. Do yourself a favor by having a strong rebuttal prepared for each of their potential lines of reasoning. Of course, you know your parents best but here are a few common arguments they might make—along with some rock-solid responses that will have you living rent-free and 10 grand richer in no time.

> **Your Folks:** "You're in the real world now, honey. We don't *need* the extra money but it's time for you to learn some responsibility. This is tough love. Trust us, you'll thank us 10 years down the road for forcing you to learn financial responsibility and restraint early in life. There is no free lunch."
>
> **Your Reply**: "Mother, Father. I thank you for birthing me. I know that during the last 20-plus years, you have always tried to do what's best for me and I respect you greatly for this. I realize that I am now officially a member of the 'real world,' and must take on a new level of responsibility. This is one of the main reasons that I implore you to abandon this rent-my-old-room policy. I have been thinking seriously about the type of financially responsible actions I want to take and one of them is becoming a homeowner early in life rather than wasting my money renting an apartment that will never belong to me. My goal is to save the $400 a month that you are planning to charge me for rent and establish a solid financial foundation that will put me on the accelerated path to homeownership in three to six years."

> **NOTE**: Parents, and older people in general, *love* to see young people making long-term plans. A PowerPoint presentation with diagrams, flow charts and a five-year financial plan will drive your point home. Present statistics that show how being in debt is directly tied to lower rates of homeownership among young adults.

Your Folks: "Daughter, I love you to death but you are, and have always been, an expensive child. When you were in high school, your lavish lifestyle added $2,500 worth of discretionary costs to my annual budget. When you went to college, you became even more expensive as four years of tuition payments and non-stop contributions to your ever-decreasing pocket money fund has left me considerably grayer and poorer. I finally have the chance to be free of your financial dependence and now you expect to move back in. I doubt this will be just a free-rent deal. You will expect me to feed you and clothe you and put gas in your tank like I did when you were in high school and I'm just not interested."

Your Reply: "Mother, I want you to know that I am very thankful for every hour you put in at work and every dime you have spent to make sure my life was comfortable and my opportunities were numerous. Now that I'm a young adult and a little more wise to the ways of the world, I realize just how good I had it growing up and how much I took your love and the financial support from your hard-earned paycheck for granted. That's why I have decided that, when I move back, I will not to be a liability to you, but an asset. You can expect me to act more or less like a part-time hired hand. I will run errands for you (help you fix that leaky faucet or bake those brownies for your office Christmas party). I will also use my digital expertise to simplify your life in ways that you could not even imagine (list ways). I plan to give as much as, or more than, I take in this arrangement." (If you have siblings living at home, even better. Offer to be their live-in tutor and college prep counselor.)

Your Folks: "Oh no. You are not going to be one of those bum-children still living at home in your mid-30s and dependent on your parents for all your needs. I love you too much—and

I spent too much on your education—to let you remain a child psychologically."

Your Reply: "Parents, I understand (and appreciate) your concern, but this setup is truly temporary and the underlying purpose of my return proves this. I do not plan to use the money I'm saving on rent to buy the latest video games or the cutest outfits. I have chosen the more responsible option of (insert: starting an emergency savings fund, putting money into my 401(k) plan, paying off my student loans and credit card debt, etc.).

HOW TO DEAL

So you decided to move back home and you convinced your parents to let you stay for little or no rent. Congratulations.

But living with your parents is still *living* with your *parents* and you still have to cope with the loss of your autonomy, independence and personal space.

Do these few things to cope, and your life will be infinitely better.

THE $15,000 YEAR ENDORSES...

The Sleepover. You're living at home so why not relive one of the best experiences of your pre-college years: The sleepover. Spend a weekend hanging out at a friend's place. Pack a couple changes of outfits and head to said friend's apartment Friday after work and stay until Sunday. This is a perfect option for those weekends when you plan to stay out late. Offer to buy your friend dinner or fill their gas tank and they'll be more than happy to host you tri-weekly.

The "Staycation:" Homebody Edition. This is a variant of the sleepover but it involves complete freedom, solitude and personal space. Instead of crashing on a friend's couch, you spend one weekend every couple of months at a decent hotel in town (check online for special deals). Or, even better, convince your parents to take a trip together—tell Dad to accompany Mum to that upcoming business conference this year. Then you'll have the place all to yourself. These periodic stints of independence should be just enough to get you through those particularly stressful times of the year.

Texting. If your parents aren't already texters, put them up to speed on this optimal communication method for the iLifer living at home. Texting allows you to check in with your folks and ease their minds without having to excuse yourself from company or give away too many unnecessary details when you're out trying to be a spontaneous young adult. A simple "Im ok ill b home in a coupl hrs luv ya lol" will do the trick.

The Talk. Use this time to really engage with your folks and pick their brains for knowledge and guidance. Now that you're officially a working adult, you can talk to your parents about a host of things that would've soared over your head before you left for college (e.g., work issues, retirement plans, relationships). You may be surprised at how helpful they can be in facilitating your transition into the "grownup" world. Set aside one day every week or so to have dinner with them and talk about the latest. Tell them what's going on in your life and on your job. Ask them about theirs.

Getting Your Old Room Back. Your folks may have converted your room into a storage space or an office when you left for college. Offer to help them organize their things in a more efficient way (one that allows you to reclaim your old space). Offering to move some things into storage (and paying for it) might be a good option that works for both of you.

Helping Out With the Little Things. If you have a steady income, help your parents out with some of their basic living expenses. Pay for the groceries every once in a while or have your mom's car washed or her oil changed while she's napping. Even if you're not yet employed, you can help out by washing the dishes or cutting the grass without being asked. Little surprises like this will go a long way in making up for whatever inconveniences you might be causing by moving back. This tip is especially useful for those staying with aunts, uncles or family friends.

Temporarily Living at Home

I feel so strongly about this that I want to try and convince those of you who are dead set on moving out on your own to reconsider. Here's a compromise. Live at your parental home, *temporarily*. Maybe just for the summer or for a few months while you settle in at work. Or just long enough for you to put together an emergency fund or raise enough money to put down a security deposit and first and last month's rent.

Any renter will tell you that you need a nice little treasure chest of savings before you can comfortably move out on your own. Some say $3,000 or $4,000 at a minimum. Spend your time at home building this.

ANNUAL SAVINGS: ***$4,626***
(Based on staying at home for five months out of the year.)

AT HOME ALL OVER THE WORLD

The moving back movement has gone global. In France, for example, some 65 percent of people in their mid-20s are still living with their parents—double the proportion that stayed in the nest in 1975.

On Your Own

For some of you, moving back home simply is not an option because of your job location, your relationship with your parents or other prohibitive reasons. This means you'll be renting an apartment, possibly for the first time. The rest of this chapter focuses on how to find an affordable apartment, furnish it on the cheap and save tons on your utility bill.

ON LOCATION

Where you decide to live will probably have the biggest impact on your finances. It will influence your transportation costs, your grocery tab, your entertainment costs, your utilities bill and, of course, your rent. The best way to keep all of these costs down is to choose a locale with a low cost of living. This usually means a suburb or other non-metropolitan area.

Now, I realize that most urbanite iLifers have their heart set on living in a vibrant, trendy city so I won't try to convince you to rent that $350 a month flat out in the boonies for a year (even though it is *just* a year; *SAVINGS*: ***$5,122***). But you should make an informed and prudent decision, even if it means prioritizing your financial goals over your social life this year. Your decision about where you will live is probably the easiest way to tell how committed you are to completing this one-year challenge. If you decide to move to the trendiest neighborhood in a high-cost city, I can almost guarantee you that you'll chicken out of the $15K Year in the first couple of months. Don't kid yourself into thinking you will live on nothing but Ramen and Pop Tarts in order to make up for your sky high rent. Living amongst the rich is the best way to make yourself feel poorer than you are. You'll quickly find out that it's harder to keep up with the Joneses when they're pushing high-performance Ferraris.

If you have flexibility about what city you will move to, check out cost of living comparison calculators like the one at www.bankrate.com* to find out exactly what you'll be signing up or when you decide to relocate. Bankrate's calculator lets you compare two cities and see a cost breakdown for housing, healthcare, movie tickets, a two-piece chicken combo, a tube of toothpaste and a bunch of other consumer expenditures that vary by location. It'll even tell you how much income you need to have in each city to maintain the same standard of living (for example, a salary of $45,000 in New York is about the same as making $30,700 in Atlanta).

iLifers & The City

- 57 percent of young urbanites say the city is the perfect place for them.
- 45 percent of Americans between the ages of 18 and 34 would like to live in New York (only 14 percent of Americans 35 and older are interested in living in New York).
- 38 percent of young Americans wouldn't mind living in LA (only 8 percent of those over 35 want to live there).

Source: Pew Research Center, *For Nearly Half of America, Grass is Greener Somewhere Else*, 2009

Most Expensive U.S. Cities

1. New York, NY
2. Los Angeles, CA
3. Miami, FL
4. Honolulu, HI
5. San Francisco, CA
6. Chicago, IL
7. White Plains, NY
8. Houston, TX
9. Boston, MA
10. Washington, D.C.

Source: Forbes.com, *America's Most Expensive Cities*, 2008

*Click on the "Calculators" tab, then follow the "Personal Finance" link to find the "Cost of Living Comparison Calculator."

Here's a list of the Top 10 cities for recent college grads. *Forbes* compiled this list based on average starting salaries, cost of living, percent of population with college degrees, expected job growth and percent of adult population in the 20 to 29 age range. Apparently, Texas is the place to be.

BEST U.S. CITIES FOR RECENT GRADS

1. Houston, TX
2. Dallas, TX
3. Austin, TX
4. Denver, CO
5. Seattle, WA
6. Atlanta, GA
7. Charlotte, NC
8. Raleigh-Durham, NC
9. Washington, D.C.
10. San Francisco, CA

Source: Forbes.com, *Best Cities For Recent College Grads*, 2008

IN THE NEIGHBORHOOD

If you've already landed a job in a particular locale, your major decision will be what neighborhood to live in. No sugarcoating here: If you want to pull off the $15,000 Year, you probably won't be living in the hottest district downtown. These areas are reserved for people who are quite wealthy (or posers ear-deep in debt) and downtown dwellers usually pay unbelievable premiums to live at the center of all the action. As someone trying to establish the kind of financial security that will allow you to buy (not rent) one of these well-positioned condos in the future, paying a "scenery tax" this year is not an option.

But the good news is that the iLifer life stage is the best time to live in a less expensive location. You don't have to worry about education opportunities for your children, you're too young to get upset over a little ambient noise and, if you consider yourself to be street-smart, you can move to a low-income neighborhood without stressing about the safety of a child or spouse. Additionally, contrary to what we see on Wisteria Lane, most upper-middle class communities are fairly unsociable. If you want to actually know who your neighbors are, live in a ward where there's a greater sense of community. This will also make it easier for you to find ways to volunteer your time and engage in social service. Plus, when you're old you'll have some pretty cool stories to tell about that one time when you *almost...*

CONSIDER THE COMMUTE

If you'll be driving to work, try to find an affordable apartment that's close to your job. The payoffs could be massive. According to the American Automobile Association, it cost an average of 17.9 cents per mile to operate a medium-sized car in 2008 (i.e., the cost of gas, maintenance and tires). This means you could save more than $900 per year by living five miles away from your job instead of the national standard of 15 miles. That's $75 per month. In addition to curbing your carbon emissions and having more free time, you can pocket $900 of your $15,000 savings simply by living closer to work (assuming that housing costs are comparable). Living close to your job is preferable to living near the best entertainment spots or your favorite restaurants because you drive between home and work 10 times a week while you patronize food and fun spots much less frequently.

ANNUAL SAVINGS: $930

(Plus 130 hours, or 5+ days, not sitting in traffic)

HOW TO FIND THE PERFECT APARTMENT FOR THE PERFECT PRICE

So you've decided to move out on your own and you've picked a city and (maybe) a neighborhood. Now, it's time to find your pad for the next 12 months.

If you're a graduating dorm-rat who has only lived in on-campus residence halls or university-sponsored apartments and will be moving into your own place for the first time, there are a ton of things you'll need to know. I'll cover some of the basics here but this can be an extremely complex process so be sure to conduct some independent research and get guidance from your older siblings, friends, co-workers and parents.

THE VIEW

Ask these important questions via email or over the phone before you decide to see an apartment:

- **Availability.** Make sure the advertised units are still available.
- **Price: What's included?** Verify that the price quoted is still valid. Also, ask what is included in the rent, what the details of the security deposit system are and what other "hidden" costs are associated with the apartment (application fee, setup costs, cleaning fees). Tell them you don't want any surprises and they'll usually be straight with you. You can even ask what the last person who moved in to that apartment had to pay in total upfront costs.

Avoid renter's regret by asking all the important questions before signing your lease:

- **What are the average costs of utilities?**
- **What is the parking allowance?** Are there additional costs?
- **What are the rules regarding changing, modifying or painting the apartment?**
- **What are the available amenities** (e.g., gym, swimming pool, tennis courts, community center, etc.)? The more of these things you have in-house, the less you will have to spend for the "Entertainment" part of your budget (See Chapter 11).
- **Try to see the exact apartment you will be living in.** Not a "model" room or a "comparable" unit.
- **Get the low-down on what the place is really like** (i.e., what the landlord isn't going to tell you). Talk to people in the building or check online forums anonymously. There, you'll see candid testimonials of people who hated the place and people who absolutely loved it, giving you the scoop on crime, insects, ambient noise and what the landlord is really like. Trust, the building owners are doing a thorough background check on you. Flip the script and make sure *they* are legit. Visit sites like www.apartmentreview.net or www.apartmentratings.com to hear the good, the bad and the ugly.
- **Appliances.** Does the place come with a dishwasher? Is there a laundry facility in the building? If not, how far (and how cheap) is the closest Laundromat?
- **Are pets allowed?**
- **Do a walkthrough.** Check to make sure everything in the apartment works and is in decent shape (check for carpet stains, chipped paint, hot water, etc.).

THE LEASE

Before signing, look over your lease with a parent, guardian or anyone else over 30 that you trust. You can do this in person or by email. This is usually a pretty surefire method for avoiding most of the pitfalls associated with the contract process and it really is a must. Your folks, unlike the person trying to fill a vacancy in his building, have your best interests at heart.

But even before you consult your parents, confirm the following details of this crucial tenant-landlord agreement:

- **Know what is due each month and when it is due.** And "how" it is due. What forms of payment will your landlord accept? Is there a grace period? And if so, how long is it?
- **Past-due penalties.** Know how much you will be charged if your rent becomes past-due or your check is returned.

GUARD YOUR SECURITY DEPOSIT WITH ALL YOUR MIGHT!

Your security deposit is supposed to be a deposit, not an extra month's payment. Know the terms surrounding whatever deposits you make. Check with your renter to find out exactly what is meant by "ordinary wear and tear," which will not eat away your SD and "damage," which will. Ask for detailed descriptions of previous scenarios in which people lost part or all of their security deposit. Obtain a written receipt of your deposit and a written list of existing damages. When you move out, you are entitled to a written itemized list of any damages and/or rent owed.

- **Maintenance.** Who is responsible for maintaining the heating, a/c, plumbing and appliances?
- **What are the penalties for breaking the lease?** And how much notice you have to give before you move out?
- **Moving out.** Are there any special requirements you have to meet before you move out (professional cleaning, carpet shampooing, etc.)?
- **What are the conditions for lease renewal?**

ON THE MOVE

Tips for Keeping Your Moving Costs Down

- Get moving boxes for free. Ask your local grocery store or hardware store for spares.
- Use old newspapers instead of bubble wrap.
- Pack it yourself. Instead of paying movers to pack up your things, invite your friends over and have a packing party. Buy everyone lunch and offer to help them pack on their moving days.
- Move it yourself? You could save hundreds in one day by bypassing the professional movers and moving all your stuff independently.

NEGOTIATE!

In the world of renting, absolutely everything is negotiable. Relatively. Be polite, be assertive and, most importantly, be informed about the market and you could save and extra $500–$1,000 this year. Because of the recession, many landlords who usually don't negotiate are cutting deals. See if you can get an extra $50 or $90 slashed off the rent or a month free.

NOTE: Check out www.rentometer.com to get an estimate of what other people in the neighborhood are paying.

ROOMMATES

Unless you're making way more than the average starting salary for grads or living in a town with über-cheap housing costs, you're most likely going to have to live with a roommate in order to meet your target expenditure in this category.

But it's really not as bad as it might seem. Think of it as getting a $3,500 raise for living with a friend for one year. When you include the costs of cable, Internet, utilities and insurance, you could be saving even more.

I'm not going to say anything about the importance of finding a roommate that suits your personality and living standards. After four or more years of college, you already know that the decision about who to share your living space with is not one to be taken lightly. You know whether or not you can live with a semi-naturist who has hygiene issues or a snorer who breaks things when intoxicated, so I'm going to assume you will be very careful about who you decide to room with during this year.

But I do want to talk about the importance of choosing a roommate with a *financial* personality that is in tune with your $15K Year commitment. Ideally, you'd want to find someone willing to do the $15,000 Year with you and provide a little positive peer pressure to save cash and stay committed. But, if that's not possible, you're going to want a roommate with these qualities:

1. **Financially Responsible.** Both of your names will be on the lease and if your roommate fails to pay rent or trashes the place, you both will face penalties (e.g., losing your security deposit, having to pay late fees). A financially irresponsible roommate can also mess up your credit by bouncing checks or "forgetting" to send a check to the cable company.
2. **Generally Frugal (or at Least a "Frugality Ally.")** This basically means someone who is not averse to saving money and who will be generally open to your dollar-stretching ideas for furnishing the apartment (see below), buying groceries (See Chapter 10), and entertainment (See Chapter 11). Rooming with an impulse buyer or shopping addict might influence you to be more carefree about your spending and renounce your budget diary ways.

The iLifer's Guide to Furnishing Your Crib

If you're moving into your first apartment, chances are you will be responsible for transforming it from a drab domicile of four bare walls into a stylish, eccentric abode that embodies your unique persona and artistic flair. Or at least four bare walls with a couch. Either way, furnishing your apartment can be a lot of fun or really expensive. Unless you're making Hollywood money, it cannot be both.

Here's a list of the essentials, along with sample costs, based on low-end prices at furniture king IKEA:

ITEM	SAMPLE RETAIL COST
Mattress Bed	$479
Sofa/Couch/Futon	$499
TV Stand	$209
Table and/or Desk	$89
Coffee Table	$89
Chest of drawers	$149
Curtains or blinds	$39
Chair	$179
Lamp	$29
Bookshelf	$80
Trash Can	$8
Shower curtain and rings	$10
Dishware, cookware, cups and utensils	$189
Refrigerator	$698
Dining Table + Chairs	$149
TOTAL	**$2,800+**

Below is a list of your $15K-Year-approved options for furnishing your new place. They are ordered from most desirable (read: cheapest) to least desirable (read: pocket burners). Follow this guide and you could stash away more than $2,000 of your yearly savings:

1. **Pilfering From Your Parents and Relatives.** As we saw in the last section, before the Great Recession, Baby Boomers were notorious

for their consistent luxury spending. One of the side effects of this is that, over the years, they have amassed a whole lot of stuff that they no longer use. This is perfect for the iLifer looking to save a couple grand on furnishing his or her first pad. Ask your parents, grandparents, aunts, older cousins and family friends if they have any unused or unwanted furniture or dishware. An even better option comes from Kristen Gustafson, author of *Graduate!*:

> *"Invite all your relatives over, and make them sit Indian-style on the floor while you serve them Ramen noodles on paper plates. I guarantee that within a week you'll have more furniture than you can handle—and possibly a few cookbooks. It's amazing what people have stored away in their basements and attics."*
>
> —KRISTEN GUSTAFSON, *Graduate!* (2002)

See how many of the above furniture essentials you can secure for free using this method before going to the next option.

ANNUAL SAVINGS: $1,772

2. **Thrift Stores and Second-Hand Stores.** Thrift shops such as Goodwill and the Salvation Army have also benefitted from America's growth and profligacy over the past few decades. When people find themselves running out of space in their garages, they pack up truckloads of long-forgotten furniture and make donations to second-hand stores.

   These socially conscious retailers offer great prices on well-built, vintage furniture that can really give your place a one-of-a-kind vibe. Instead of maxing out your credit card to get that furniture set from *Entourage* or *Sex & the City*, head to Goodwill and get the set from *Mad Men* or *I Love Lucy*. With a little style and creativity, you can create a unique and nostalgic atmosphere that still has the Hollywood feel, even if it's Hollywood circa 1959. Embrace the retro theme for a year while you build up your savings. If at the end of the year you decide that the $40 couch from 1975 no longer suits you, you can sell it on Craigslist for 20 bucks (or donate it back to Goodwill) and buy a new, contemporary set with cash.

   TIP: "Shop early in the week for best selection, following weekend clean-out-the-garage donations." —Jeff Yeager, *The Ultimate Cheapskate's Road Map to True Riches* (2008)

TIP: Ask the sales associate about upcoming "special sales" days the store will be having. These stores tend to have storewide 50-percent-off days and you could save a bundle just by shopping on the right day of the week. If you have already found what you want and you're worried you'll lose your *Brady Bunch* coffee table if you wait three days until the sales day, ask the associate if they'll hold it for you. They usually say yes.

ANNUAL SAVINGS: ***$1,866***

3. **Craigslist.** One beautiful thing about the 21st century marketplace is the ability to find a seller who has exactly what you want and nothing more. Check sites like Craigslist (the "free" link!), Uloop, and eBay as well as www.freecycle.org, where all items are free.

   ANNUAL SAVINGS: ***$1,073***

4. **Garage Sales.** Before taking the retail route, see what you can pick up at local garage sales. Look out for signs posted in the neighborhood as well as under the "garage sale" link on Craigslist and www.garagesalehunter.com.

   ANNUAL SAVINGS: ***$1,205***

NOTE: In addition to being $15K Year friendly, all of the above options are environmentally friendly as well. They extend the functional lives of items and keep them out of the waste stream. A theme you'll run into occasionally throughout the rest of the book: Live green, save green.

5. **Discount/Big Box Stores and IKEA.** If you must buy new furn, head to one of the major discount stores. IKEA is a top-drawer destination for handsome minimalist wood, steel, and plastic products with $15K-Year-friendly price tags. Check out IKEA's selection of "slightly damaged" merchandise where the savings are even more cordial.

   ANNUAL SAVINGS: ***$587***

6. **Regular Stores.** Taking a visit to a local or chain furniture store can take a toll on your bank account and, since the above options work so well for young and creative independents, such a practice is not endorsed by this book. But, if you feel you must, at least try to barter for a great deal while you're there. First, find out which store is having the biggest sales and go there. Then, haggle like it's 2009. Take advantage of a buyer's market and exploit your opportunity to be a fussy consumer. Ask for a deep discount, request to buy floor models and find out whether the store will

beat prices you find elsewhere. The worse they can do is say no and, when they do, that's your cue to head for the door.

ANNUAL SAVINGS: ***$215***
(but only if you haggle!)

7. **Other Options:**
   - *Campus Diving*. If you're reading this anytime before or during the early May to mid-June commencement period, fire up your laptop and find out when the colleges in your area have their move-out days. Head to campus and help yourself to any of the discarded futons, microwaves, bookshelves and office chairs that appeal to you. *ANNUAL SAVINGS*: ***$179***
   - *Curb Shopping*. One man's trash is another man's dresser. Head over to the affluent side of town and see what the Richistanis have tossed out as they've traded up. Check the Web for trash pickup days. *ANNUAL SAVINGS*: ***$338***
   - *Dishes*. During the 1980s and 1990s, and even now, a lot of Americans took up the strange practice of buying fancy dishware that nobody used. In recent years, these unused dishes have made their way to garage sales and thrift stores all over the country and can be bought for as low as $1 or $2 per set. They are perfectly useful for your purposes and many of them are as good as new. *ANNUAL SAVINGS*: ***$38***
   - *Cutlery*. Stores like McDonald's, Subway and BK have unbelievably low prices (read: free) on plastic utensils (and napkins). I'm lovin' it. Grab a handful with your Big Mac (but make sure you re-use these and reduce waste). *ANNUAL SAVINGS*: ***$20***
   - *Dollar Stores*. **CREATIVITY CHALLENGE:** Take $30 and go to the best dollar store in town. Buy 25 things that can be used for furnishing or decorating your pad. You may be surprised at just how far a buck can go. *Hint*: pick up kitchen accessories, cleaning materials, and decorative trinkets and toys. *ANNUAL SAVINGS*: ***$78***
   - *DIY*. See what you can make for yourself. Whether it's fashioning a faux-nightstand out of a moving box and a bed sheet or constructing a coffee table out of wine crates, there are a lot of furniture basics and decorative pieces that you can create DIY style. Hit the web for advice on how to pull this off (www.thriftyfun.com). *ANNUAL SAVINGS*: ***$139***

RESOURCE: Take a look at *The Cheap Bastard's Guide to the Good House + Home* (2007) for tips on how to furnish every room in your apartment for less.

Utilities

The average consumer unit under the age of 25 spent $1,069 on "utilities, fuels and public services" in 2007, excluding telephone services. Using the tips below, try to reduce your energy costs by 40 percent or more this year. These tips can help you save the planet and up to $655 this year by greening your apartment.

ENERGY DRAINERS

According to the 2007 Buildings Energy Data from EnergySavers.gov, the most expensive sources of energy in a typical household are:

- Space Heating (31 percent)
- Space Cooling (12 Percent)
- Water Heating (12 percent)
- Lighting (11 percent)
- Appliances (9 percent)
- Computers and Electronics (9 percent)
- Refrigeration (8 percent)
- Other (8 percent)

GETTING STARTED

Audit. A home energy audit can identify ways to save hundreds of dollars a year on home heating (and air conditioning). Ask your electric or gas utility if they audit homes for free or for a reasonable charge. If they don't, ask them to refer you to a qualified professional.

Enrolling in load management programs and off-hour rate programs offered by your electric utility may save you up to ***$100*** a year in electricity costs. Call your electric company for information about these cost-saving programs.

HEATING, COOLING AND LIGHTING

HEATING

Adjust your thermostat. To 68 degrees during the day and 60 degrees at night. You can save 3 percent on your heating costs for every degree you reduce the temperature below 70 degrees for the entire heating season. *ANNUAL SAVINGS:* ***UP TO $95***

Turn down your thermostat at night. Or when you're away for more than four hours during the day. If you're in a chilly climate, don't turn off your heating system entirely as this may cause pipes to freeze. *ANNUAL SAVINGS: $77*

Install a programmable thermostat. You can program it to turn your temperature way down or up when you're at work or sleeping. These cost around 50 bucks and could save you ***$130*** a year.

Check the ductwork for air leaks. Check for leaks about once a year if you have a forced-air heating system. To do this, feel around the duct joints for escaping air when the fan is on. You can repair relatively small leaks by covering holes or cracks with duct tape. More stubborn problems may require caulking as well as taping.

Use kitchen, bath and other ventilating fans sparingly. You can blow away a houseful of heat in just two to three hours using ventilating fans. Turn them off when their job is complete.

Dress warmly. The human body gives off heat about 390 BTUs per hour for a man and about 330 BTUs per hour for a woman. Dressing warmly can help you retain natural heat. Wear closely woven fabrics, which add at least a half-degree in warmth. Slacks are at least a degree warmer than skirts; a light, long-sleeved sweater equals almost 2 degrees in added warmth; a heavy long-sleeved sweater adds about 3.7 degrees; and two lightweight sweaters add about 5 degrees in warmth because the air between them serves as insulation to keep in more body heat. *ANNUAL SAVINGS: **UP TO $145***

Test your windows and doors for air tightness. Add weather stripping and caulk where necessary. It's low-cost and can save you 10 percent or more in annual energy costs.

Use the ceiling fan for heat.

> *"In the winter, reverse the motor and operate the ceiling fan at low speed in the clockwise direction. This produces a gentle updraft, which forces warm air near the ceiling down into the occupied space."*
>
> —ENERGYSTAR.GOV

*TOTAL ANNUAL SAVINGS: **UP TO $240***

COOLING

Set your thermostat at 78 degrees. This is a reasonably comfortable and energy efficient temperature.

Chill out. Don't set your thermostat at a colder setting than normal when you turn your air conditioner on. It will not cool faster, but it will cool to a lower temperature than you need and use more energy.

Don't place lamps or television sets near your thermostat. Heat from these appliances is sensed by the thermostat and could cause your system to run longer than necessary.

Clean or replace air conditioning filters. Air filters should be cleaned or replaced every month.

Keep out the daytime sun. Place vertical louvers or awnings on the outside of your windows. Draw any draperies, blinds and shades.

Turn your lights down low. Keep lights low or off when not needed. Electric lights generate heat and add to the load on your air conditioner.

Light cooking. Cook and use other heat-generating appliances in the early morning and late evening hours whenever possible.

TOTAL ANNUAL SAVINGS: ***$102***

LIGHTING

Go with CFLs. Try replacing some of your regular incandescent bulbs with compact fluorescent lights. They use 75 percent less electricity than traditional bulbs and they'll last about 10,000 hours (10 times longer than incandescents). They are more expensive but they pay for themselves many times over during their lives.

Get out more. Spend more time outside of the house and be sure to turn your lights off when you leave.

Solar Energy. Open up the dirty window; and let the sun illuminate...

Turn lights off when you leave a room. Even if you'll just be gone for a sec.

TOTAL ANNUAL SAVINGS: ***$52***

IN THE KITCHEN

COOKING

Never boil water in an uncovered pan. Water will come to a boil faster and use less energy in a kettle or covered pan.

Match the size of the pan to the heating element. More heat will get to the pan, and less will be lost to the surrounding air. Get in the habit of turning off the elements or surface units on your electric stove several minutes before completing the allotted cooking time. The heating element will stay hot long enough to finish the cooking without wasting electricity.

Turn off the oven five to 10 minutes before cooking time is up and let trapped heat finish the cooking.

Multi-bask. When using the oven, cook as many foods as you can at one time.

Avoid opening the oven door repeatedly to check food that is cooking. This allows heat to escape and results in the use of more energy to complete the cooking of your food. Instead, watch the clock or use a timer.

Use pressure cookers and microwave ovens. They save energy by reducing cooking times.

Thaw frozen foods before cooking. This will save time *and* energy.

*TOTAL ANNUAL SAVINGS: **UP TO $100***

DISHWASHER

Bust some suds. Instead of putting your dishes in the dishwasher, try washing dishes by hand. This method uses less hot water and electricity. According to Pacific Gas & Electric Co., running a load of dishes in your dishwasher costs $0.37 per load if you have an electric water heater, or $0.16 per load with a gas water heater.

Scrape dishes and rinse with cold water before loading them into the dishwasher. Avoid using the dishwasher's pre-rinse cycle.

Don't use the "rinse-hold" on your machine for just a few soiled dishes. It uses three to seven gallons of hot water each time you use it.

Fully loaded. Be sure your dishwasher is full but not overloaded when you turn it on.

Let it air dry. Air dry dishes instead of using your dishwasher's drying cycle.

*TOTAL ANNUAL SAVINGS: **UP TO $61***

REFRIGERATOR

Don't keep your refrigerator or freezer too cold. Recommended temperatures: 38 to 40 degrees Fahrenheit for fresh food compartments of the refrigerator; 5 degrees Fahrenheit for the freezer compartment.

> NOTE: To check the temperature on older refrigerators, place an appliance thermometer in a glass of water in the center of the refrigerator. Read it after 24 hours. To check the freezer temperature, place a thermometer between frozen packages. Read it after 24 hours.

Regularly defrost manual-defrost refrigerators and freezers. Frost buildup increases the amount of energy needed to keep the refrigerator at its proper temperature. Never allow frost to build up more than one-quarter of an inch.

Hot & Cold. If possible, avoid placing your refrigerator or freezer in direct sunlight or near the stove.

Make sure your refrigerator door seals are airtight. Test them by closing the door on a piece of paper or dollar bill so it is half in and half out of the refrigerator. If you can pull the paper or dollar out easily, the hinge may need adjusting or the seal may need replacing.

*TOTAL ANNUAL SAVINGS: **UP TO $80***

CLOTHING

LAUNDRY

Wash clothes in warm or cold water. Rinse in cold.

Fill washers and clothes dryers but do not overload them.

Keep the dryer's lint screen clean and its outside exhaust free of obstructions. Clean the lint screen after each load of laundry, and check the exhaust regularly. A lint screen in need of cleaning and a clogged exhaust can lengthen drying time and increase the amount of energy used.

Use the old-fashioned clothesline. It's enviro-friendly and it can make clothes seem fresher and dryer than those emerging from a dryer. According to PG&E, an electric dryer costs $0.40 per load, and a gas dryer costs $0.13 per load.

TOTAL ANNUAL SAVINGS: UP TO $73

IRONING

Remove from the dryer and hang clothes that will need ironing while they are still damp.

Steam Power. Save energy needed for ironing by hanging clothes in the bathroom while you're bathing or showering. By doing so, you can steam some wrinkles out and cut down on ironing time.

Avoid piecemeal ironing. Save energy by ironing large loads of clothes at a time.

TOTAL ANNUAL SAVINGS: UP TO $31

TOTAL ANNUAL UTILITIES SAVINGS: $655

CLOSING NOTE ON HOUSING

Remember, housing is by far the most expensive expenditure for most Americans. Cutting back in this area is the easiest way to pull off the $15,000 Year. By living at home or renting a low-cost apartment, you'll save thousands and set yourself up for early homeownership. You can pocket an extra few hundred bucks by picking up inexpensive furniture and monitoring your utilities use this year.

CHAPTER 9

TRANSPORTATION.

"You are who you are,
No matter how fast,
Your money or your car."
—M.I., TALK ABOUT IT (circa 2008)

SPENDING BREAKDOWN

iLIFER: STAN D'ARD

CURRENT: Pre-$15,000-Year Expenditures
ANNUAL: $7,952*
MONTHLY: $663

TARGET: $15,000 Year Expenditures (**GOING CAR-FREE**)
ANNUAL: $2,054
MONTHLY: $171

TARGET: $15,000 Year Expenditures (**WITH A CAR**)
ANNUAL: $4,360
MONTHLY: $363

SAVINGS: **$3,592–$5,898**

Based on figures from the 2007 Consumer Expenditure Survey, our standard iLifer currently spends about 20 cents out of every dollar on transportation, for a total of $7,952. While this is slightly less than the $8,121 average annual cost of car ownership estimated by the American Automobile Association (AAA), the pre-$15K-Year expenditures stats above leave plenty of room for improvement. This chapter focuses on reducing transportation costs and in the next few pages you'll find information about how to live car-free or car-lite, how to buy your first car $15,000-Year-style and how to save $1,000+ on gas this year.

*This breaks down into $3,200 in car payments, $2,028 for gasoline and motor oil, $504 for maintenance and repairs, $567 for vehicle insurance, $253 in finance charges and $1,400 for air travel.

Fast Money, Fast Cars...

First of all, for those of you who already have a car—great. If it works, no need to buy a new one. Because transportation costs make up such a large chunk of your budget, avoiding all the setup fees, registration costs and financing charges associated with purchasing a vehicle is crucial to accelerating your road to $15,000 savings. Holding on to your current car is basically the only way to do this*. Sorry. But, to make you feel better, here is a calculation of what you'll save by postponing your car purchase for a year: ***ANNUAL SAVINGS*: *UP TO* $2,016**†.

Hopefully, that figure was a spoonful of sugar to all you car owners who were set on trading up this year. Unless you're willing to sell your car and go auto-free for the year (***ANNUAL SAVINGS*: $4,500 *TO* $5,500**), feel free to skim past the next few pages, which are directed at those without cars. Later in the chapter, you'll learn how to cut your gas bill down by $1,000 and a few other tips for keeping your transportation costs down this year.

CAR-FREE LIVING

Now, if you currently don't have a vehicle, the first thing I'm going to do is try to convince you to go without a car for a year (or for as long as you can hold out).

Wait, where are you going? Before you toss the book over your shoulder and head to the dealership, hear me out. I'm going to expose an oily little secret that car salesmen and the entire auto industry have worked very diligently to conceal.

When it comes to cars, to buy or not to buy is a question you will ultimately have to answer for yourself. But, before you succumb to the sly pitch of an experienced salesman or the sensuous purr of a new engine and empty your account, realize that **owning a car usually costs *twice* as much as buying a car**. Automobiles come with thousands of dollars worth of unavoidable expenses that most potential buyers disregard once they see a sticker price or misleading monthly note that they consider manageable.

According to a 2008 report by AAA, the average American pays $8,121 to own and operate a car over the course of a year. That's a

---

*According to CNN, four out of five people were planning to keep their car longer because of the recession.

†Financial planners say that people who keep their cars for 10 years rather than five, will save more than $250,000 over the course of their lives.

little more than $675 a month. Your car payments and insurance premium are just the beginning of the "True Cost to Own" (TCO), which the auto experts at www.edmunds.com have defined as the total operating, ownership and maintenance costs over a period of five years. Their TCO calculator takes into account insurance, financing, taxes, fees, registration, gas, maintenance and repairs to tell you exactly how much currency is coming out of your pocket to pay for your vehicle—and it's typically double the sticker price. Take a click for yourself and put in the information for the car you want to buy and see what you'd really be signing up for.

For a little more motivation to keep reading, think about the fact that the average American spends 51 hours each year sitting in bumper-to-bumper traffic and that automobiles are the single largest cause of air pollution in the United States. Oh, and don't forget that auto accidents are the leading cause of death for young people between 20 and 29.

Now, I wouldn't throw all of those stats at you simply to make you feel bad and not give you an out. Contrary to what $20 billion in auto advertising would have you believe, for a large portion of the population, it is entirely possible to live a fulfilled and productive life without owning a car.

While doing the research for this book, I read Chris Balish's *How to Live Well Without Owning a Car**. Balish exposes the idea that every American is supposed to have a car for the advertising-induced†, profit-driven myth that it is. With testimonials from more than 100 happily car-free individuals all over the country, he makes a strong case in defense of his argument that buying a car is often the worse financial decision a lot of Americans make.

But the best part of his book is his in-depth description of the steps you can take to "live well without a car." Step One: Ask yourself these questions:

1. **Can you get over your own ego?** For $8,000, I say you can.
2. **Can you get to work without a car?** Point Blank: "If you can get from your home to your place of employment and back safely and on time without a car, then you probably don't need to own one" (Balish, 2005).

---

*This is a really good book. Take a look at it even if you have your mind set on buying a car (or if you already own one). To save money, see if you can pick it up at the library or click through it on Google Books.

†The automotive industry spends more money on advertising than any other industry in the country.

3. **Do you live in an urban area, or in a mixed-use development?** (Read: Are you young, employed and between the ages of 21 and 27?)
4. **Do you have access to public transportation?** According to U.S. Census records, 49 percent of Americans live near a transit stop. This number is even higher for iLifers, who tend to migrate to urban areas in overwhelming numbers.
5. **Do you live in close proximity to amenities?** Based on my personal research, there's a Wal-Mart, McDonalds, CVS, AT&T, Bank of America and Home Depot within a one-mile radius of every stoplight in metro America.
6. **Are you flexible?** Well, are ya?

Aside from number 2, the idea of being "flexible" is the most pertinent one for iLifers. You're in the best position to take some seemingly extreme actions and try some things that are completely off limits to your elders (in a few years, they'll be outside of the realm of possibility for you, too). Capitalize on the fact that you don't have kids to chauffer to school and karate practice, your body is still lithe enough to bike for a mile and you feel completely comfortable sitting next to someone who doesn't look like you on a train. Using the options below, test out car-free life for two weeks (***Savings*: $312**) before deciding whether or not to buy a car.

OPTIONS FOR CAR-FREE LIVING

1. **Mass-Transit.** Let someone else drive you to work while you get your multitask on. Read, iPod, text, people watch and/or check up on the latest gossip blogs on the way to work for maximum efficiency. With more buses and trains offering Wi-Fi than ever before, public transit has become the "IT" thing to do. ***Annual Savings*: $5,120**

   > *"Public transportation produces 95 percent less carbon monoxide (CO), 90 percent less in volatile organic compounds (VOCs), and about half as much carbon dioxide (CO2) and nitrogen oxide (NOx), per passenger mile, as private vehicles."*
   >
   > —WWW.PUBLICTRANSPORTATION.ORG

2. **Carpooling and Ridesharing.** With social networking on the rise, the chances of you connecting with that one person who lives and works near you and keeps similar hours are higher

than ever. *ANNUAL SAVINGS*: ***$3,852*** (assuming you offer to buy gas for those who drive).

3. **Motorcycle.** Your annual motorcycle ownership costs could be lower than $2,000. ***ANNUAL SAVINGS: $4,530***

> *"Life may begin at 30, but it doesn't get real interesting until about 150."*
> —Author Unknown

4. **Biking.** It's healthy. It's green. It's cheap. And it's doable. In *Go Green, Live Rich,* David Bach notes that 40 percent of the trips we take in our cars are for distances shorter than 2 miles. *ANNUAL SAVINGS*: ***$5,490***

5. **Car Sharing.** If you live in an urban area, check out car-sharing companies such as ZipCar and Flexcar, which have expansive operations in major cities. With annual costs usually under $1,000, car sharing is a lot easier and cheaper than you might think. Google it. *ANNUAL SAVINGS:* ***$5,232*** (based on average Zipcar user).

6. **Car Renting.** Even if you rent a vehicle every other weekend to run errands or to go out, you'll still save thousands on transportation relative to car owners. At $80 a weekend, you'd spend about $2,000 over the course of a year. Enterprise will even pick you up. *ANNUAL SAVINGS*: ***$4,122*** (add another ***$754*** to that by using widely available online discount coupons for rental companies).

7. **Make Your Errands Come to You.** One blissful thing about the 21st century is the ability to take care of errands such as banking, bill payment, apparel shopping and even grocery shopping from the comfort of your laptop.

Combine the options above (along with the occasional practice of bumming a ride from friends) and you might be surprised at how flawlessly you can operate without a money-devouring car. Even if you can't last the whole year, going car-free for three or six months quickly adds up to thousands in savings (***$3,188*** for six months).

> *"Since I gave up owning a car I am now totally debt-free, I'm saving an amazing 50 percent of my income and I'm on track to retire at age forty-five. Plus I live a more fulfilling life. And I still get everywhere I need to go with ease."*
> —CHRIS BALISH, *How to Live Well Without Owning a Car* (2005)

As a final motivation to take the car-free plunge, check out this cost comparison by Dallas native and author of the blog *Living Car-Free in Big D**.

To Car or NOT to Car

Posted on Wednesday, January 21, 2009 at 07:02AM

Let's examine how much I save in transportation costs since loosing myself from the vexing finger-cuffs at the hands of Toyota, shall we?"

CAR-RELATED EXPENSES	AMOUNT/MONTH
Buying/Leasing a new car	$300
Down payment (prorated)	$200
Insurance	$150
Parking (at Interurban building)	$120
Gas	$40
Airport parking	$15
Taxes, Tags and Fees	$30
TOTAL	**$855**

CAR-FREE EXPENSES	AMOUNT/MONTH
Monthly DART pass	$90
Cab fees	$30
Airport carfare	$15
Occassional rental car (prorated)	$35
TOTAL	**$170**

Buying a new car would have cost this Texas-based blogger $10,260 over the course of a year. He saved more than *$8,000* by opting to go car free for the year. Check out the resources below for more information about car-free living.

THE $15,000 YEAR ENDORSES... www.walkscore.com.

Go to www.walkscore.com and put in your address. This website is a great mapping tool for locating services near almost any location. It'll help you find the nearest movie theatres, restaurants, grocery stores, fitness centers and more for your address. The higher the score, the easier it will be for you to live without a car.

*carfreeinbigd.blogspot.com

RESOURCES

Car-sharing Websites
www.zipcar.com
www.flexcar.com
www.citycarshare.org
www.carsharing.net

Carpooling Websites
www.erideshare.com
www.carpoolworld.com
www.carpoolconnect.com

Car-Free Websites
www.carfreeamerica.org
carfreefamily.blogspot.com
carfreeinbigd.blogspot.com
www.carfreechicago.com

TO THOSE WHO MUST BUY A CAR

Unless you have loads of cash sitting around and no debt to speak of, buying a brand new car right now will not put you on the road to financial freedom. But, to make you feel better about leaving that new car on the lot, realize that, had you bought it, it would've lost 20 percent of its value as soon as you drove away from the dealership due to depreciation.

Listed in order from least expensive to most pricey, here are your $15K-Year-safe options for buying:

Go *Old*-School. Get a *Nick and Norah's Playlist*-style Yugo (or comparable classic) for **$500–$2,000**. If you just need something that will get you from point A to point B (hopefully the two points are quite close to one another), search for a car with character. And by character, I mean 100,000+ miles and a very loud air conditioning system. There are obvious drawbacks to purchasing a car that is nearing the end of its life cycle, but it *is* kinda modish in a weird way and you're likely to get a one-year crash course in auto maintenance that will save you thousands during the course of your life. More importantly, there are tons of ways to find solid older cars and hedge yourself against the potential challenges that come with buying a clunker. Each state has consumer protection laws for car buyers, or "lemon laws," which protect consumers from shady salesmen. If, after conducting thorough consumer research, the 1988 Cadillac you bought still turns out to be a lemon, contact your State Attorney General's Office for help getting your dealer to repair your car or reimburse your money. And don't forget to sound the consumer alarm by posting a scathing review of your dealer on sites such as www.dealerrater.com.

> NOTE: www.lemonlawamerica.com provides information about state and federal lemon laws.

ANNUAL SAVINGS: ***$4,227***
(With a few extra repair trips taken into account.)

Buy a Late 20th Century Car. And hook it up with a few 21st century touches. Although a lot of decent cars built in the mid- to late 1990s can be had for less than $5,000 or $6,000, there's a good chance that driving that 1998 Chevy Malibu won't be the most pleasant experience unless you pimp your ride with a few 21st century conveniences. Integrate your iPod with your stereo system ($10-$100). Install power door locks for keyless entry ($75). Get a portable GPS system ($99) or use your cell phone's navigation service ($0). Buy seat heaters to keep your bum warm ($79). Get in contact with your mechanic to make a few minor performance upgrades. Make these changes and you can whip your whip into 21st century shape with less than a grand. (This is also a good strategy for those who already own a car but want to buy a more modern one.)

ANNUAL SAVINGS: ***$2,058***

Buy a Lightly Used Car. Also known as a "new used" car. Consider getting a vehicle that was new only a few years ago and has less than 50,000 miles on it. If you're taking this route, check out Certified Pre-Owned Cars, which offer extended warranties and a little more peace of mind than the above options.

NOTE TO GRADS

A new car is a common parental gift for students graduating from college. Parents often pay for the car but leave the graduate with an insurance bill, vehicle registration fees and other associated costs. An option: Ask your parents to get you a gently used car instead of a brand new one as long as they agree to pay for all of the associated fees.

ANNUAL SAVINGS: ***$1,341***

6 THINGS TO DO BEFORE BUYING A USED CAR*

1. Head to www.edmunds.com and www.fueleconomy.gov to compare the "true" prices of the various models you're interested in. Edmunds.com will give you the True Cost to Own while fueleconomy.gov will let you know what you can expect your annual gas bill to be (as well as your annual greenhouse gas emissions). Both of these sites allow you to compare multiple cars at once so they're a great resource to start out with (cars with similar sticker prices can have ownership prices that differ by thousands of dollars).

2. Check the most recent *Consumer Reports* buyer's guide for a list of the most reliable used vehicles (and the models to avoid). The crew at CR does a great job of researching the best and worst of what you'll find on used car lots and provides separate lists based on your target price. Below, there's a list of some of the top models in the $4,000 to $6,000 range. See www.consumerreports.org for the latest details.

3. Once you've looked up a couple dealers with decent prices on cars you like, compare the seller's asking price with the average retail price in the Kelley Blue Book (www.kbb.com), which tabulates a vehicle's worth based on the model, year, mileage and specifications of the car you're interested in. This number is to be your upper limit when it comes to negotiation.

4. Get the car inspected by an independent mechanic. It'll run you about $75 to $125 but it's well worth it. The mechanic will tell you what repairs you can expect to make in the years ahead.

5. Pony up $20 or $30 for a vehicle history report based on the car's VIN number. Sites such as www.autocheck.com or www.carfax.com will put the number through a database to determine whether or not the car has been damaged by accidents, fires or flooding and whether it has been returned to the dealer as a "lemon" in the past.

---

*Disclaimer: This is not an extensive list. Purchasing a vehicle is a major financial decision and these are just a few of the steps you should take.

6. When you've found a car you're interested in buying, go to the dealership with an experienced adult who knows what to look out for. If possible, try to bring someone who can drive a hard bargain. This person will also be able to alert you to potential red flags and hidden costs that you might not be aware of.

MOST RELIABLE USED CARS
(1998 and later)
Price Range: $4,000 to $6,000

Each of these cars earned better- or much-better-than-average ratings in CR's 2008 survey. (Prices are based on "typically equipped models with average mileage.")

- 1999 Acura CL
- 1998 BMW 328i Sedan
- 1999–2001 Ford Mustang (V6)
- 1999–2000 Honda Accord
- 1999–2000 Honda Civic
- 1999–2000 Infinity G20
- 2000 Mitsubishi Eclipse
- 1999–2001 Mazda Protégé
- 2000 Nissan Xterra
- 1998–1999 Toyota Camry
- 1998–1999 Toyota RAV4

Source: *Consumer Reports* Buying Guide 2009

ONE OF THE BENEFITS OF BUYING USED

Most people pay thousands of dollars in interest and financing charges when they buy a new car. By using the methods above (not buying a car or buying a less expensive one), you can avoid the interest trap. Spend the year taking public transit or driving that 15-year-old car (with character) while you build up enough credit to get a great car loan rate or enough cash to put down a 50-percent down payment. You can cut your interest payments by more than half and save thousands on a car if you simply delay gratification until you can afford it.

Car Insurance: iLifer Savings Strategies

The average American spends about $1,000 on car insurance every year and, since insurance companies see young people as high-risk drivers, iLifers usually get stuck with crazy-high premiums. One of the best ways to save on auto insurance is to get older but, in the meantime, follow these tips and you'll cut your insurance costs by a couple hundred bucks this year.

Keep Your Driving Record Clean. Drive safely and make sure there aren't any old blemishes on your driving record (check with the DMV). This could save you hundreds over time.

Boost Your Credit Score. This is another area where your FICO score may come into play. Some insurers use your credit history to determine what kind of risk you are. A better score could lead to a lower premium.

Hit the Web for the Best Rates. Check out sites like www.esurance.com, www.insure.com and www.geico.com to compare prices and read customer reviews. All insurers are not created equal.

Check with the State. Your state's insurance department offers comprehensive price comparisons. Visit the insurance department website for your state (e.g., www.insurance.ca.gov). Navigate to the consumer division and look for the page with auto insurance comparisons. Some insurance departments provide customer complaint statistics for each company.

Raise Your Deductible. By increasing the amount you agree to pay for repairs after an accident, you'll decrease your monthly premium (for example, raising your deductible by $500 will save you about 30 percent). If you have an older car, it may be wise to drop the collision coverage. Check your car's blue book value to see whether or not collision coverage is worthwhile.

Drive a Cheaper, Less Flashy Car. High-performance cars produce more expensive premiums because they have high repair costs and are more likely to be stolen. Visit the Insurance Institute for Highway

Safety (www.iihs.org) for a list of cars with the highest "theft claim frequency" and see which cars not to buy.

TOTAL ANNUAL SAVINGS: **$272**

10 Ways to Save $1,000 on Gas this Year

According the CES, the average household spent $2,384 per year on "gasoline and motor oil" in 2007. Most people can save $1,000 or more every year by making a few minor adjustments on the road. Use the tips below to reduce your gas bill (and your carbon emissions) this year and give your savings account a fill up.

THE CAR

1. **Go Car-Light.** Remove unnecessary junk from your car as well as car racks and other items of considerable weight. You'd be surprised at what an extra 50–100 pounds can do to your gas consumption rate. *ANNUAL SAVINGS*: **$75**
2. **Keep Your Tires Properly Inflated.** Inflating your tires can be done at most gas stations or when you take your car in for a checkup. Properly inflated tires are also safer and last longer. *ANNUAL SAVINGS*: **$63**
3. **Get a Tune Up.** Keep your engine properly tuned and your mpg will thank you. *ANNUAL SAVINGS*: **$82**
4. **Check and Replace Your Air Filters Regularly.** This also protects your engine from damage. *ANNUAL SAVINGS*: ***UP TO $175***

THE DRIVER

5. **Shop Around.** You can save dozens of dollars by comparing prices at different stations, pumping gas yourself, and using the lowest octane called for in your owner's manual. Websites like www.gasbuddy.com and various cell phone apps will tell you where the cheapest station in your area can be found. *ANNUAL SAVINGS: $75*
6. **Stop Driving Like a Maniac.** This is the most important tip. Driving casually and avoiding aggressive moves, such as fast accelerations and slamming on the brakes, can improve your fuel

economy by a combined average of 42 percent, according to Edmunds.com. That means savings of more than $600 for someone who drives 15,000 miles a year, gets 20 miles to the gallon and pays an average of $2 a gallon. *ANNUAL SAVINGS: $630*

7. **Take it Slow for a Year. Drive the Speed Limit.**

> *"You can assume each 5 mph you drive over 60 mph is like paying an additional $0.24 per gallon for gas."*
>
> —WWW.FUELECONOMY.GOV

*ANNUAL SAVINGS: $160**

8. **Use Cruise Control.** This helps you maintain a steady speed and cut back on accelerating too much—provided you're on a flat road. *ANNUAL SAVINGS: $49*

9. **Drive Less.** Use some of the "Options for Car-Free Living" to save a bunch by going car-lite. Each week, skip one car-trip: take a walk, ride a bike or see how far you can thumb your way down the Info Superhighway. *ANNUAL SAVINGS: $187†*

10. **Work Your Windows.** Running the air conditioner can cause your car to drink gas faster, but driving with the windows down causes drag on your car and decreases its efficiency. On the highway, use the a/c. Around town, roll the windows down. *ANNUAL SAVINGS: $38*

Visit www.fueleconomy.gov for more tips

TOTAL ANNUAL SAVINGS: $1,121–$1,498

Flights

The CES does not specifically report on airline ticket purchases but let's assume our standard iLifer normally takes about one non-work-related flight every three months, or four flights per year. Travelocity says customers paid an average of $338 for each round-trip domestic ticket leaving in April 2009. Assuming you are a little more cost-conscious than the average flyer, I'll round that number down to $300 per flight. But that still leaves you with $1,200 in ticket fees— you can add

*Add $290 for the speeding ticket and traffic school fees you'll escape this year.

†Bikers and walkers, add another $252 for cancelled gym membership, and avoided diet book costs.

another $200 for baggage fees, on-flight food and drink, rebooking fees and other extra costs. Air travel total: **$1,400**.

In terms of getting that number significantly lower, there aren't too many fancy tricks that I'm going to offer you. I'm going to give you the benefit of the doubt and assume that, since you came of age in the age of aggregator sites and email price alerts, you know how to scour the Internet for the cheapest fares and have updates sent to your Blackberry once a ticket price drops. You already know that buying your tic 21 days in advance and flying on Tuesdays, Wednesdays and Saturdays will save you loads. You already know all about student discount programs such as Airtran's X-fares (www.airtranU.com), which allows travelers under the age of 23 to fly standby for $69 per segment. You probably know about all of the following sites, most likely others as well, which tend to offer the best deals on air travel:

www.kayak.com
www.sidestep.com
www.farechase.yahoo.com
www.farecast.live.com

The one thing I can tell you to do is to save money on flights the old-fashioned way—by keeping your feet on the ground (and your head out of the clouds). Try as much as possible to cut that four-trip total down to two trips during the $15,000 Year. Invite your old college friends to come to visit you. Have your family meet you for Thanksgiving and fly home for Christmas. Postpone that trip to Miami until next year. Take the bus or the train or carpool. See if you can schedule a free trip using your reward miles.

Flying has become extremely stressful over the past few years so save yourself a few headaches and a bunch of cash by going jet-lite this year.

ANNUAL SAVINGS: ***$600***

See Chapter 11 on Entertainment for more information on budget travel.

CHAPTER 10

FOOD.

"Eat breakfast like a king,
lunch like a prince,
and dinner like a pauper."
—ADELE DAVIS

SPENDING BREAKDOWN

iLIFER: STAN D'ARD

CURRENT: Pre-$15,000-Year Expenditures
ANNUAL: $5,295
MONTHLY: $441.25

TARGET: $15,000 Year Expenditures
ANNUAL: $2,424
MONTHLY: $202

SAVINGS: **$2,871**

So, we're down to the last of the Big Three: Food. Of the basic necessities—shelter, transportation and sustenance—this is the one where young Americans tend do the most overspending, regularly forking over huge premiums at the grocery store and in restaurants for foodstuff they could have picked up for a fraction of what they paid. But the bright side of this is that it's entirely possible to cut your food bill by 60 to 70 percent without making any major lifestyle changes or quality sacrifices. In the 21st century marketplace, the savings go to the savvy and this chapter will start you on your way to getting your grub on for less.

iLifers and Restaurants

There's a lot of evidence that suggests that busy, kitchen-shy iLifers are frequenting restaurants and take out spots more often than most:

- Mintel International's 2009 American Lifestyles study found that, among all age groups, 18- to 24-year-olds were most likely to say they were spending *more* on fast food and dining out despite the recession.
- In 2005, FastFoodSource.com reported that 20-somethings were more likely than any age group in history to eat outside of the home.
- The National Restaurant Association (NRA) says that Americans eat 4.2 meals per week (or about one out of every five) in a commercial setting. This translates to about 220 meals per year (about 40 percent of these are sit-down meals and the rest are takeout). At 5.2 away-from-home meals per week, young people have the highest rates of eating out and, not surprisingly, young males (18–34) lead the pack, clocking in at nearly 6 commercial meals a week.

Let's see just how much this is costing young folks. For convenience, I'll round the NRA's number down to five meals per week, which breaks down nicely into two sit-down and three takeout meals (104 and 156 per year, respectively). At the conservative prices of $15 per sit- down meal and $5 per takeout meal, we're already at $45 per week, or $2,340 per year.

Simply by cutting your out-of-home meals down to one dine-in meal every other week and two takeout meals per week, you could save more than $1,500 over the course of the year. That's the first and probably the simplest food savings recommendation of the $15K Year. Cut back on eating out. I'm not saying anything new here and every middle-aged financial planner will tell you the same thing. And, while I hate the idea of sounding like a 46-year-old personal finance-head, I can't ignore the obvious. According to the BLS, 44 cents out of every dollar spent on food in the United States in 2007 was spent in a restaurant, making dining out at least twice as expensive as eating at home.

Cut your restaurant visits down to a maximum of twice a month (24 times a year) and your Chinese takeout trips down to twice a week max and your bank account will be well fed.

Disclaimer: This rule should not apply to those of you who have found food "gems" in your neighborhood—places where you can get a decent meal for under $4 (or a large-portion meal for under $8, provided you can stretch it into two meals). Pizza spots, sandwich joints and "buy one get one" promotions are common gems. The best gems are the ones near your place of work that allow you to take a low-cost lunch break and escape the walls of your office for an hour. If you have discovered such a venue, feel free to become a regular there.

ANNUAL SAVINGS: ***$1,518****

This is just the tip of the iceberg when it comes to savings. The following blogpost by my friend Miss Moneypenny offers an itemized account of what you can save by avoiding restaurants:

If it makes you FAT and costs MONEY, DON'T DO IT

Posted on Sunday, January 11, 2009 at 10:42PM

My resolution for this year—if it makes me fat and costs me money, I shouldn't do it. That means no Chick-fil-a biscuit in the morning on the way to work. Lunchtime french fries? Adios. I mean it. Really, what could be a bigger waste of money per unit? Think about all the unintended costs of those deceptively delicious fries? Let's count them, shall we?

1. The Fries: $1.50
2. The Gas to get to the Fries: $0.75
3. The Gym time needed to work off the equivalent of the 300 calorie fries: $20
4. The new Jeans I need to buy because of weight gained from fries: $100
5. The Therapy session I will need to combat my low self-control: $75

TOTAL*: *$197.25

Ergo, New Years resolution—save money and my... well you know.

But, once again, I wouldn't just tell you to stop going out to eat without giving you an out. Here's a list of $15K-Year-approved alternatives to that overdone and overpriced practice of dining out:

1. **Bring the Restaurant Atmosphere Home**. Invite a few friends for a home-cooked dinner at your place (but not too many unless you

*Based on replacing the out-of-home meals with food prepared using the USDA's December 2008 low-cost food plan for 1-person families (and reduced gas costs).

feel comfortable handing them a bill at the end of the night). Or you could do pot luck (call it something else when you send out the email or text to the attendees). Play background music. Dim the lights and fire up some candles. Floor mats?

PROS: You get to create the restaurant vibe that suits your tastes and control the music playlist. You don't have to keep your voice down. You don't have to give subtle hints to try and get the attention of your waiter when your drink goes empty. You don't have to leave a tip. Even if you cook all of the food yourself, this is still less time consuming than a trip to the diner—you save time by not driving all the way to the restaurant, not waiting to be seated, and not waiting for the increasingly long food prep time that most restaurants now have.

ANNUAL SAVINGS: ***$1,094***

2. **Bring the Restaurant Atmosphere Home (2.0).** If you don't want to cook or do potluck, you could get takeout and set it up at your "home restaurant," just ordering the main items (beef, chicken, etc.) and supplying the sides (e.g., rolls, salad) and the drinks yourself. Once you subtract the tip, the garnishes and the beverages (and take into account a reduced price for takeout), you'll probably save anywhere from 30 to 50 percent. If there's free delivery, you could save an additional $2 to $8 on gas by not leaving your house. Even if delivery isn't free, use a fuel cost calculator to find out how much your trip to the restaurant would cost you. If the delivery charge is less than (or about the same as) the number in the calculator, then order in and get started on preparing the sides so everything will be ready once the deliveryman arrives.

   NOTE: Most restaurants have full menus online so you can decide what to order from the comfort of your apartment.

   ANNUAL SAVINGS: ***$799***

3. **Old-fashioned Takeout.** Dining in tends to be more expensive than ordering to go. Pick up takeout from your preferred restaurant and eat it at home (no restaurant atmosphere needed).

   ANNUAL SAVINGS: ***$550***

4. **Do Dessert-and-a-Movie Instead of Dinner.** Grab a bite at home and then meet up with your friends for ice cream at your local scoops shop. Then head to the theater—or, even better, to a friend's place to watch a DVD. (This is also an awesome date idea. Don't worry, your date will see it as creative, not cheap.)

   ANNUAL SAVINGS: ***$90–$120***

5. **Food for work.** Pack your lunch to work (leftover pasta is usually a good option), but don't spend your lunch hour in your cubicle or in the drab cafeteria of your office. Head to a local park and eat that chicken sandwich or spend the first 10 minutes eating indoors before walking over to that museum that always closes before you leave the office. Instead of spending half of your lunch period driving to a restaurant and waiting 20 minutes for your meal to be prepared, save money (and your sanity) by getting out of the office and doing something rejuvenating in the middle of the day. You can even take a quick afternoon nap.

ANNUAL SAVINGS: ***$1,075***

The strategies above will help you save by simply reducing your away-from-home food consumption. But, as a young socialite, spending some time eating in a commercial setting is inevitable. Here are a few ways to save money while eating out.

1. **Never Buy Drinks with Your Meal.** Always order water in a restaurant. Drinks are heavily overpriced (and much less healthy). Or bring your own drink. It may not seem like the "classiest" thing to do but you should ask yourself who benefits from this definition of class? Clearly, it's the corporate restaurant big shots (and the beverage retailers) who get to charge you a 400 percent markup for a glass of flat soda when you could easily pick up a half dozen cans at a convenience store around the corner for the same price. One of the very few upsides of a recession is that you can reject all kinds of expensive etiquette norms without paying too many social costs.

   ANNUAL SAVINGS: ***$125***

2. **Tipping.** A solid 17 percent tip should be a standard, even for a cheapskate. Throw in a few extra percentage points for a really good waiter that enhances your overall dining experience. Don't try to "eyeball" it—take your cell phone out and use its calculator. The eyeballing method (or its cousin the "round up" method) will cause your tips to be out of whack, rewarding poor service with a 20 percent tip or confusing and discouraging a great waiter with only 12 percent. Also, check to see if the tip has already been included in your bill (this often happens for large groups).

3. **Specials Treatment**. Ask your waiter if the eatery has any secret specials or coupons that you should know about. If he gives you inside information and helps you save money, give him an even bigger tip.

4. **Hungry? Wait.** Fast once a month, simply not eating anything before dinnertime. Not only is this a good way to build self-discipline, it'll give you a small glimpse into what most people on the globe experience regularly: Hunger.

   ANNUAL SAVINGS: $88
   (Take that money and donate it to an organization that fights world hunger.)

5. **Play the AYCE.** Skip lunch and then stuff yourself at an all-you-can-eat buffet. These are great options because you never have to wait for prep times and you can feast on a great variety of foods at one price. But, be sure to get your money's worth.

   ANNUAL SAVINGS: $177

6. **To-go Plates.** At the risk of sounding like your mother: Never leave food on your plate. Even at a restaurant. Ask for a "to-go" plate and stretch an extra meal out of the leftovers. You may be so stuffed that the idea of eating another bite disgusts you but, trust me, when you get the midnight munchies two days later and your refrigerator is barren, you'll be happy to have a Styrofoam savior that you can toss in the microwave. Restaurant leftovers are also good for making stir-fry, omelets and a bunch of other quick meals (and the to-go plates are often reusable).

   ANNUAL SAVINGS: $78

7. **BOGO Plates.** Make a two-month pact to patronize restaurants with coupons (exclusively). "Buy one entrée get one free" coupons tend to be the best. Check online to see if your preferred restaurant or fast-food joint has a coupon floating around on the Web. If you're on a date and you're too embarrassed to be seen using a coupon, then discreetly slip the BOGO pass behind your credit card in that little black folder-book-thing with the credit card-holder when you get the bill. Don't forget to tip on the *pre-discount* total.

   ANNUAL SAVINGS: $60

8. **Free Food!** Festivals, meetings, grand openings, receptions, art gallery exhibitions and college campuses often have free grub. To make sure the event promoter's idea of "Food Provided!" doesn't mean tummy teasers or thin crackers, call ahead. If you're too embarrassed to ask what's on the menu, simply ask the event coordinator "Who's catering?" and then call the caterers to ask what they'll be serving at the event in question. Also, a lot of these events have trouble gauging what turnout will be like so

they either have too much food or (less often) not enough. If there is more food than there are people, grab a to-go plate before you leave.

ANNUAL SAVINGS: ***$49***

9. **Eat Late, Eat Cheap!** Many delis and sandwich shops offer up to 50 percent off original prices if you show up within a couple hours of closing. Peruse your neighborhood to find out which shops have policies like this and time your arrival perfectly every time.

ANNUAL SAVINGS: $52

SHOW UP LATE, EAT CHEAP!

Step One: Eat at home.
Step Two: Join your friends at the restaurant just in time for dessert.
Step Three: Order the ice cream or a slice of cake.
Step Four: Spend the rest of the evening out on the town with the crew.
Step Five: Pad your pockets with the 15 bucks you just saved.

10. **Splitting the Difference.** If all your friends ordered the $17 steak and you had a $10 chicken salad, you could end up paying a 45 percent "split-bill" tax if you don't speak up. Instead of splitting the bill, ask the waiter for separate checks or do the math on your iPhone app of choice.

ANNUAL SAVINGS: ***$21***

The iLifer's Guide to Grocery Shopping

Twenty-first century grocery shopping doesn't have to be stressful or time-consuming. Use the following tips to pwn the grocery store and save loads of dough, cheese, bread and lettuce.

I. DIVERSIFIED MARKETS: WHERE TO SHOP

Wally World. Consumer research shows that Wal-Mart is king when it comes to food shopping as it has become the most popular destination for food purchases in the country. You may or may not be a fan of Wal-Mart but its low prices, one-stop shopping experience and ubiquity make it a cost-effective choice for the $15,000-Yearer. Wal-Mart also lists per unit prices, which are key for comparing costs (See section on per-unit pricing below).

Major Supermarkets. Stores such as Kroger, Safeway, Ralph's, Publix and Supervalu. Most of these grocers offer free loyalty-club programs that are relatively easy to sign up for (and can save you a bunch). Be sure to check the weekly specials of these stores before deciding which one to patronize. They're usually available online (See "Web 2.0 Meets the Grocery Store" below for info on using the Web to find deals).

Warehouse Stores. At stores like Costco, Sam's Club and BJ's, products are packaged in large quantities and the costs per unit tend to be much lower than alternative options. They'll charge you about $50 for a membership (split it with your roommate or a friend) but the savings will usually pay you back in the first few visits. For its November 2008 "Live Cheap" issue, *New York* magazine compared the costs of 53 different grocery items across four different grocery stores. They found that the final total at Costco was $101 while the bill at three other grocers ranged between $279 and $281, making the warehouse store about 65 percent cheaper than other options. (The other stores were Gristedes, Whole Foods and Food Emporium.)

> NOTE: Warehouse stores also sell much more than food. You can find discounted prices on everything from car tires to contact lenses to gasoline.

Drug Stores. Check out their weekly sales items, which can be found online or in the Sunday paper. Stores like Walgreens, Longs Drugs and CVS fall into this category.

Dollar Stores. Great for toiletries, trinkets and personal products at the hard-to-beat price of a buck. One of the most overlooked savings options.

Ethnic Shops. We are the most diverse generation after all. Be about it. Check out your neighborhood Cuban, Korean, Ethiopian, and other community marketplaces and shops. You'll find that everyday staples like rice, beans, veggies and meats tend to be cheaper and you get to expand your palette by experimenting with new spices and flavors.

Farmers' Markets. Depending on where you live, it may be possible to get fresh produce at ridiculously low prices by attending farmers' markets. These urban bazaars usually set up on the weekends and have become quite popular during the last 15 years*. They offer deals on everything from apples to zucchini. To find a farmers' market near you, ask around or go to www.localharvest.org and click on "Markets."

By taking advantage of the above options, you can develop a strategic, diversified approach to grocery shopping and save up to 60 percent on your food bill.

*ANNUAL SAVINGS: **$2,809***

II. WEB 2.0 MEETS THE GROCERY STORE

With Web 2.0 technology, there is no reason you should ever pay "regular" prices for any major grocery item. There is also no reason you should ever spend more than 30 minutes in any particular store. Skillful surfing will direct you to the best deals in your city and keep you from wasting time perusing the contents of each aisle, looking for deals. Here are just a few of the hundreds of Web-based methods for saving on groceries:

Have a List. I know, you've heard this advice before. You've likely ignored this advice before as well. But, a list is really your only way to combat the sensory overload that occurs whenever you set foot in a modern supermarket. Today, the average grocery store contains more than 30,000 items, two-and-a-half times as many as it did 20 years ago. Without a solid list, you're two-and-a-half times as likely to over-shop, overspend and be sticker-shocked when the cashier rings up your total. From the music to the store layout to the lighting, the 21st century supermarket has been strategically designed by consumer psychologists and crafty architects to make shoppers spend more time and more cash than they bargain for.

But the good news is that there are all kinds of 21st century methods for combating these schemes. Coming up with a Web-based grocery list is one of the easiest ways to save time and money at the market.

Start by choosing one or two major grocers and clicking through their websites (a great way to kill time at work). Most stores offer virtual weekly ads that allow you to create a shopping list based on the sale items of the week. Open the virtual ad, then click on the items that have the best sales and add them to your virtual shopping list. Once you've clicked through the ad online, you'll have an automatically generated

*The number of operating farmers' markets grew from 1,755 in 1994 to 4,685 in 2008.

shopping list based on the items that you singled out. Print it out or send it to your PDA and just like that your shopping list is ready in less than three minutes. This also cuts down your in-store time because you don't have to wrestle with a large, awkward newspaper ad in the store to find out what's on sale or go up and down each aisle to find the best deals. Armed with your store-specific list, you can pinpoint the items you need and get in and get out.

ANNUAL SAVINGS: ***$585***

Loss Leaders. These are those products listed at such ridiculously low prices that stores actually lose money by selling them. They usually can be found on the front page of a store's weekly circular or under headers such as "Super Coupons!" or "Buy One Get Three Free!" Grocers use these to lure in customers, hoping that when you buy other items on your shopping list, you will overspend so much that the store makes up for whatever it lost on loss leaders at the end of the day. When you see such deals, your plan should be to stock up on these discounted items without buying too much else (thus, beating the stores at their own game). Using aggregator websites such as www.MyGroceryDeals.com and www.GroceryGuide.com, it is entirely possible to pick up everything on your list at loss leader prices. Doing so can cut your total grocery bill by as much as 70 percent! (See "Deal or No Deal" section below for help identifying loss leaders.)

ANNUAL SAVINGS: ***$1,388***

THE NEW COUPON: BACK. AND BETTER THAN EVER.

> *"There's an entire sect of cheapskates—Couponeers—who are dedicated almost exclusively to competitive grocery shopping. You've seen one in the grocery store before. The typical Couponeer is a slacks-clad woman, age thirty to fifty-five, with a pregnant-looking envelope full of coupons tucked securely in her grocery cart and on a string around her neck a pair of school kid scissors (her weapon of choice for spur-of-the-moment in-store clipping). On double-coupon days Couponeers are out in force. On rare triple-coupon days they can be downright dangerous."*
>
> —JEFF YEAGER, *The Ultimate Cheapskate's Road Map to True Riches* (2008)

Yeager's description of "Couponeers" highlights the distinction between 20th century savings methods and the convenience-driven coupon culture facilitated by the digital age. A small but growing number of iLifers have come to realize the cost-cutting power of technology and young, tech-savvy savers are at the forefront of transforming the age-old process of discount via coupon. As the digital coupondom encroaches upon the traditional model, the process of saving money at the supermarket is becoming simpler, more user-friendly, more collaborative and more consumer-empowering.

COUPONS.... *DON'T CALL IT A COMEBACK!*

- Coupon use is re-gaining popularity. For the first time in 14 years, coupon redemption didn't decline in 2007, according to NCH Marketing Services. A 2008 survey by ICOM Information & Communications found that 67 percent of U.S. consumers said they were more likely to use coupons during a recession.
- Coupons.com, the world leader in digital coupons, saw record growth in 2008. More than 38 million consumers printed coupons over the course of the year, doubling the amount of savings from 2007. The site saved consumers more than $300 million in 2008 and had set a goal for $1 billion in savings in 2009.
- The number of households that get coupons from the Internet has increased by 83 percent since 2005, according to a 2008 study by Scarborough Research, a firm that tracks American consumers and what they buy.
- The number of people who only use online coupons grew 51 percent in 2008, says Simmons Market Research Bureau.
- A 2008 poll found that 61 percent of consumers in America report using more coupons now than ever before in their lives.

The average consumer stands to save more than $2,000 a year using online coupons. Below are a few ways to get your piece of the billion-dollar savings industry in one of the most coupon-friendly atmospheres of all: the grocery store.

Load Coupons Onto Your Loyalty Card. A growing number of grocers are completely digitizing the savings circuit by allowing customers to load the coupons of their choice onto their store club card. Today, you can cut out the cutting from the process and swipe your savings into existence. This is perfect for combining store coupons with manufacturer promotions from P&G eSaver. Sometimes, items can be bought for only a few pennies (or even for free) using coupon combos. As of early 2009, Kroger, Ralphs, Safeway and Giant Eagle were the main supermarkets offering this option but others were expected to follow suit. (Check out www.pgesaver.com and www.shortcuts.com for more details.)

The Grocery Game. Every week, the team at "The Grocery Game" comes up with a flawless list of the top savings at major supermarkets and drugstores across the country. TGG lets you know when an item is at its rock-bottom price and provides all the coupons you'll need to save tons. As a warning, this service isn't free. But, depending on where you live, it may be your ticket to triple-digit savings on your monthly grocery bill. Try it out. A four-week trial membership costs $1. Eight weeks of the service will set you back $10. (Visit www.thegrocerygame.com.)

Coupon Kiosks. CVS allows shoppers to swipe their loyalty card at an in-store kiosk and receive a personalized list of coupons based on their purchase history.

Be on the Lookout for... Cell phone coupons. This is apparently the next big thing in the coupon world. According to Juniper Research, a United Kindom-based market researcher, marketers expect mobile coupons to generate $7 billion annually by 2011 (See www.cellfire.com).

III. A Few Old-Fashioned Ways to Save Your Shekels At Ye Ole Market

Twenty-first century technology is great, but, in the grocery store, those with old-school, time-honored shopping skills still win out. Try out these tried-and-true savings methods at the supermarket and you could save thousands.

Compare Per-Unit Prices. Contrary to what most of us grew up believing, the "total price" isn't the most important number associated with a grocery item. That distinction goes to the "per-unit price." Most major stores provide both the total price and, in smaller type, the cost per ounce, pound or unit (at Wal-Mart, the per unit price is listed in an orange box to the left of the total). Because food products are often packaged in tricky and constantly changing ways, it can be difficult to compare items that are different sizes or shapes. For example, in the drink section, which is really cheaper: a 20-ounce Gatorade for $1.29 or two 32-ounce Powerades for $3.39? Yeah, me neither. This is where the per unit label comes in handy. At $0.053 per ounce, the Powerade turns out to be about 20 percent cheaper than the

Gatorade. Most iLifer shoppers don't take advantage of the price per unit and end up spending more money than they have to*. Don't.

ANNUAL SAVINGS: ***$591***

How Could You Be So Cart-Less? If you only need to drop into the grocery store to pick up eggs and milk, ditch the shopping cart. Remember, the architects that designed the place probably made sure there would be about 10,000 items between the entrance and the items you need most. Going cart-less is your guard against getting sidetracked and ending up with a basket full of impulse purchases.

Live on the Edge. Peruse the perimeter of the store, where the healthy food resides, before checking out the boxed, prepackaged and processed fatty foods in the center. In addition to protecting your waistline from inflation, shopping around the edges is the best way to hedge yourself against rising food prices. Dairy products, fresh meats, fruits and vegetables and other low-priced staples can be found on the outer edges of most markets. This is also a great way to spend less time in the store.

Brands-with-Benefits: Discard Brand Loyalties. If you grew up in the 1980s and 1990s, most of your brand loyalties are probably the result of pervasive child marketing rather than an informed choice about which product is actually best. Don't be afraid to break away from your comfort zone and experiment with something new. Sometimes, the cereal in the bag with the name you never heard of tastes just as good as the one with the child-targeting cartoon mascot or the familiar brand image. Go with what's on sale for the lowest unit price. You may find you like the less expensive product just as well. Even if you don't, make a commitment to buy your favorite brands only when they're on sale or buy one, get one free. When your favorite childhood snack goes to half-price for the week, stock up on a half dozen boxes.

ANNUAL SAVINGS: ***$926***

WATCH OUT FOR SNEAKY SIGNS!

"Many sales tempt you to buy more than one bag or box—by touting, for example, four boxes of cake mix for $5. But rarely are you required to buy all four to get the discount. Retailers are just planting a number in your head, hoping you'll buy a lot."

—CONSUMER REPORTS, *Shop Smart and Save Big*, May 1, 2009

Go Generic This Year. Generic and store-brand products are always cheaper than name brands and are often of comparable quality.

*According to Mintel International's 2008 Budget Shopper report: *"Young shoppers are least likely to look at price per weight (44 percent report doing so)."*

Spend the year (or a few months) buying only generic products and determine which ones are just as good as the name brand and which are unsatisfactory knock-offs. In your post-$15K-Year life, you'll be a walking *Consumer Reports* guide, never again paying a premium for a mediocre product with a big name.

***ANNUAL SAVINGS*: $1,301**

Buy in Bulk. Buy the largest quantity size rather than individual portions. If you take a look at the per unit prices, you'll notice that the individually packaged chips can cost twice as much *per ounce* as the larger bag. Don't pay for individual packaging—buy the largest size that you will actually use. This also helps you save on gas (you avoid extra trips to reload on those Oreos that always run out right before you get a craving). But try not to buy more than one person can eat.

> *"Across the board, younger shoppers are most likely to 'always look for the cheapest product possible' (62 percent report doing so at grocery stores, versus 40 percent of all respondents) and to 'often buy in bulk to save money' (32 percent at grocery stores, versus 25 percent of all respondents)."*
>
> —MINTEL INTERNATIONAL, *Spending Power of Young Adults* (2008)

***ANNUAL SAVINGS*: $1,129**

IV. DEAL OR NO DEAL?

While weekly ads can be your ticket to thousands in savings, they are still ads after all—which means marketers and retailers are trying to convince you (or confuse you) to buy something that will make them a large profit. A lot of times, supposed "deals" or "super buys" are nothing more than hiked up prices marked back down to their original levels (and dressed up with bells, whistles and exclamation points). You can put lipstick on a 16-ounce pack of sliced bacon but…

Use the following guideline prices for some basic iLifer staples to find out whether to buy an item, walk away, or stuff your cart with as many as you can. Average prices are based on January 2009 figures from the Bureau of Labor Statistics' Consumer Price Index*.

BREAD, CEREAL, AND PASTA

White Bread. *Average Price: $1.41 per pound ($0.08 per ounce)*
You should be able to find a standard loaf of bread (about 22 ounces) for **UNDER $1.50**. Anything under $0.80 is usually a steal but beware of

*These prices reflect the "U.S. city average" from the BLS. Prices may vary significantly by location. Check out www.bls.gov/CPI to find specific prices based on the metropolitan area where you live.

buy-one-get-one-free deals unless you are the type to eat a few slices daily. Because of bread's short shelf-life, young, single people face the highest risk of having a half-finished loaf go stale or grow mold. As a rule, try to buy bread one loaf at a time (should last about 10 days).

NOTE: Whole wheat bread is slightly more expensive at $0.12 per ounce but skilled shoppers can find wheat at the above prices with no trouble.

Cereal. The BLS doesn't report cereal prices but try to find cereal at less than $0.10 per ounce. For a standard 15-ounce box (sizes and weights vary greatly by brand), this comes out to **$1.50**. If you run into deals offering cereal for anything less than $0.07 per ounce (about $1.05 per standard box), stock up!

Spaghetti Noodles. Pasta can be a cheap, simple and long-lasting meal for the $15K Year participant. Try to find spaghetti noodles (or any other form of pasta) for less than $0.10 per ounce (easily done with Wal-Mart's store brand). For the standard size (16-ounce) package, this comes out to **$1.60**. Usually, any buy-one-get-one-free deal is worth pursuing in the case of pasta.

NOTE: Pasta sauce can also be had at a price of about $0.10 per ounce (or **$1.60** for a 16-ounce container of Ragú).

FRUITS & VEGETABLES

The prices and availability of many fruits and vegetables often depend on where you live and what season it is. These averages from the Bureau of Labor Services offer a good starting point for what you might expect to pay. Familiarize yourself with the prices in your area and take advantage of deals offering discounts of 50 percent or more. Don't forget about your local farmers' market, which may offer much lower produce prices than the grocery store. These markets might not have per ounce prices listed but, if the prices are significantly cheaper than grocery store produce, you'll notice right away.

AVERAGE PRICE OF PRODUCE (2009)

ITEM	PRICE/LB.
Bananas	$0.63
Apples, Red Delicious	$1.23
Oranges, Navel	$0.90
Grapes	$2.17
Tomatoes	$1.66

Source: Bureau of Labor Statistics: Consumer Price Index, January 2009

Potato Chips. *Average Price: $0.28 per ounce.* Yes, I know, *potato* chips don't count as vegetables. But at the highly inflated average price of **$4.53 PER 16-OUNCE BAG**, I felt I needed to include this in the list (and this seemed like the most appropriate category). The cost of a bag of chips rose more than 30 percent between January 2008 and January 2009. That's ridiculous. Boycott?

DAIRY & EGGS

Milk. *Average Price: $3.57 per gallon.* At the beginning of 2009, whole milk was actually getting cheaper. As you read, this trend may or may not have reversed. Either way, look out for deals that offer $1 or more off the base price for a gallon in your area ($0.75 or more for a half gallon).

Eggs (Grade A Large). *Average Price: $1.85 per dozen.* No matter where you live, there will always be a sale on eggs at some grocery store. Your job is to find it and make sure it is worthwhile. Challenge yourself to find a dozen eggs **UNDER $1** (or under $1.50 for a crate of 18). As I write, Safeway in Northern California is offering a 48-hour sale for 18 Grade AA eggs: $0.97.

Ice Cream. *Average Price: $4.41 per half gallon.* The BLS reports ice cream by the traditional size of "a half-gallon" tub but, buyers beware, for the last couple of years, ice cream companies have been shrinking their containers and that half gallon you used to enjoy as a kid has been downsized to 1.5 quarts. That's 25 percent less ice cream (about four less bowls). And, naturally, the price in real dollars has actually gone up as the containers have shrunk in size.

Regardless, on any given week there are at least two brands of ice cream on sale in the frozen aisle. But it's important to be sure the "sale" price is actually a good deal. For the $15K-Yearer, a 1.5-quart tub of ice cream should not exceed **$3** (and $2 is more ideal). So, wait until your favorite brand is on sale for 50 percent off, and then buy a couple weeks' worth. Also, I know they're tempting, but especially try to avoid those pint-size* Häagen-Dazs tubs that scream "I'm too depressed to shop wisely." Based on per unit pricing, they usually cost about $10 per half gallon—more than twice the average price.

---

*In 2009, Häagen-Dazs reduced the size of its "pint" from 16 ounces to 14 ounces.

MEATS & POULTRY

Ground Beef. *Average Price: $3.16 per pound.* Beef prices vary greatly by location but, in general, try to find ground beef under **$3 PER POUND**. On days when the discount is deep, load up. Ground beef can be frozen and kept fresh for up to four months, says the USDA. It also acts as a foundation for a large number of low-price, easy-to-prepare meals.

Boneless Chicken Breast. *Average Price: $3.30 per pound.* Another staple that can vary a lot from this average depending on where you live and where you shop. Look for coupons that offer $1 or more off the regular price. Chicken can also be kept fresh for months if frozen (a good item to buy in bulk at Sam's or Costco).

Sliced Bacon. *Average Price: $3.67 per pound.* Anything less than **$3 PER POUND** is a safe bet. Under $2 is usually a good deal. Look out for buy-one-get-one free deals here—but remember, bacon can lose its freshness relatively quickly in the refrigerator. Consider freezing.

OTHER

Frozen Pizza. BLS doesn't track average prices for pizza, but this item can be a tasty, easy-to-make and cheap meal. Try to find frozen pizzas for under $0.20 per ounce. At this price, an average sized pizza (25 ounces) should run you no more than FIVE BUCKS. Load up on pizzas that come in at anything under $0.12 per ounce—or $3 for a regulation-sized pie. Throw the pizza in the oven, put together a salad while it bakes and, after 20 minutes, bring it out, slice it down the middle and you have yourself a meal. Save the other half for your lunch break the next day. Two meals for under $6. Never call the deliveryman again. **Warning:** Buying any frozen pizza for more than $0.50 per ounce (e.g., about $3.50 for a 6.1 ounce CPK Thin Crust Pizza For One) is counter-productive. You're better off staying in bed and calling the deliveryman.

Other Items. Websites like www.couponMom.com let you search coupons and specials by largest percentage saved. For most grocery items, deals that save you 60 percent or more are usually a safe bet.

TOTAL ANNUAL SAVINGS: ***$1,639***

How to Keep Your Total Beverage Expenditures Under $200 This Year

The average iLifer spends close to $1,000 per year on beverages, leaving his bank account thirsty. Save $700+ by following the tips below and your cup won't run dry this year.

Think Outside the Bottle. Drink tap water or filtered water (**PRICE PER GLASS: NEGLIGIBLE TO $0.01**). At **$0.28 OR MORE** per glass, bottled water:

> *"is 240–10,000 times more expensive than water from the tap and is subject to less rigorous testing and purity standards than tap water*. Furthermore, the bottling process consumes the energy equivalent of 17 million barrels of oil annually and wastes two gallons of water for every gallon that is bottled."*
>
> —THE CENTER FOR A NEW AMERICAN DREAM (www.newdream.org)

NOTE: Check out www.waterfiltercomparisons.com for a price breakdown of the top drinking water filters, complete with purchase price, cost of replacement cartridges and overall maintenance cost for one year of use.

ANNUAL SAVINGS: $96†

50/50. Save 50 percent on fruit drinks *after* you buy them—use the "water-it-down" approach. Instead of paying high prices for professionally watered down juice (i.e., "flavored water"), make your fruit drinks last longer by mixing them with cold tap or filtered water. Since most juice drinks (**PRICE PER GLASS: $0.60**) are loaded with sugar and high-fructose corn syrup, a 50-50 juice-water combo still tastes great (and there are half as many calories).

HINT: Hawaiian Punch is perfect for this method ($1.97 per gallon at Wal-Mart).

HINT 2.0: Use recycled water bottles for this method—shake it up! (Best if refrigerated.)

ANNUAL SAVINGS: $184

---

*In 2008, the Environmental Working Group (EWG), a non-profit that works to protect the public health and environment, conducted independent testing of 10 popular U.S. bottled water brands. EWG found 38 different pollutants in those bottled water brands, including bacteria, industrial chemicals and Tylenol, some at the same level as tap water in the nation's most polluted tap water systems.

†This number increases to more than $610 if you drink tap or filtered water exclusively for the year—also a nice way to drop 20 pounds.

Swear Off Fizzy Drinks. After six soda-free months you'll wonder how you ever drank the stuff. At **$0.75 PER CAN**, soda costs you only about three cents for each negative health effect it provides.

*ANNUAL SAVINGS: **$109***

Swear Off Hard Drinks. At MORE THAN $7 PER DRINK (on average), alcohol is by far the most expensive of the liquids. Across all age groups, those under 25 are most likely to over-index on alcohol, spending upwards of $500 per year on beer, liquor, wine and other spirits*. Spend the $15K Year alch-free and use that $500 to buy something that won't wipe out your memory or leave you with the symptoms of pregnancy (nausea, headaches, baby bump).

> **NOTE:** For those who need a little extra motivation to save $500 by not drinking, check out www.RealAge.com, a site that tells you how much older your body really is based on how much drinking you do.

*ANNUAL SAVINGS: **$507***

The Latte is Officially Passé. A recession is no time to pay absurd premiums for designer coffee (**$4 PER CUP**). In fact, there is no level of financial security that legitimates this. Drink homemade tea instead (**PRICE PER MUG: $0.05**).

*ANNUAL SAVINGS: **UP TO $328***
(It's also healthier.)

Use Powdered Milk for Cooking. The average under-25 consumer spent $103 on fresh milk in 2007 (up 30 percent since 1997). Young singles tend to run into the expiration date problem more often than most. Try a longer-lasting alternative:

> *"Powdered milk tastes a lot better than it used to. If you haven't tried it in the past few years, it's worth another taste.... It can be substituted for fresh milk in almost any recipe with excellent results."*
>
> —WWW.HILLBILLYHOUSEWIFE.COM

*ANNUAL SAVINGS: **$49†***

TOTAL ANNUAL SAVINGS: $784

---

*Twenty-four percent of under-25s reported spending more on alcohol in 2008 than they did in 2007. This compares to only 9 percent of the total population.

†Powdered milk is about 40 percent cheaper than traditional milk.

The iLifer's Guide To Cooking

Now that you have bought groceries at the best prices and filled your pantry and refrigerator with loss leaders, it's time to get your gourmet on. Don't be dismayed. Even if you've never cooked before, it's not as hard as it looks and it's a skill that will save you thousands of dollars over the course of your lifetime.

I realize that you're young and you have things to do and places to go. Spending 75 minutes slaving over a stove to prepare a meal for one is not the typical iLifer's idea of a fun Sunday night. But, that said, I'd be doing you a great disservice if I neglected the money-saving power of cooking. *ANNUAL SAVINGS:* ***UP TO $2,647***.

And there's other good news.

There are tons of 21st century ways to make the cooking experience simpler and less stressful than ever: Download the recipe for your favorite restaurant dish to your PDA. Follow the steps of a meal-making tutorial on Youtube. Sit next to the stove and watch *The Daily Show* on your laptop while your casserole heats up. Dance to your "Food-themed" playlist while you chop onions*. We are a generation of multitaskers and, although a certain level of focus is absolutely necessary in order to ensure safety in the kitchen, it's entirely possible to cook appetizing cuisine without devoting hours of your undivided attention to a one-track task.

Many iLifers have already picked up on this as data from the 2007 Consumer Expenditure Survey show that those under 25 are spending less on eating out and cooking more at home. This trend may be a result of rising food prices, but there are other factors at work as well. Learning how to cook a fast, tasty and hassle-free meal has never been easier. Free recipes and video tutorials can be found with a few clicks and there are even websites that will come up with personalized recipes based on the items you have in your refrigerator. Cooking shows like *Top Chef* and *Hell's Kitchen* have spurred an increased interest in culinary culture and have re-conceptualized cooking as an entertaining hobby rather than a chore. Finally, the idea of eating out has become less appealing as gas prices have risen along with the prices and preparation times of most restaurants.

**Eat It* by Weird Al, *Beans & Cornbread* by Louis Jordan, that *Chili's Baby Back Ribs* jingle and *Peanut Butter Jelly Time!* by The Buckwheat Boys are good options.

8 QUICK, EASY, AND, MOST IMPORTANTLY, *CHEAP* RECIPES FOR THE HUNGRY ILIFER ON THE GO:

For those of you who are content spending the $15K Year eating nothing but Ramen ($0.48 per meal), frozen pizzas ($2.50), cereal ($0.37), Tuna Helper ($1.07), PB&J sandwiches ($0.87), mac-and-cheese ($0.88) and Omelet Surprises ($1.22), please, be my guest*. But, there is a way to reduce your food bill by $1K without eating like a college student. If you want to use this year to save cash while developing your culinary skills and actually eating well, check out these recipes (and the websites below for hundreds more). None of these recipes require fancy cooking equipment, obscure ingredients or more than 35 minutes of your time.

1. BBQ Chicken Fingers (Ready in 20 minutes; Makes 4)

3 boneless skinless chicken breasts
2 Tablespoons BBQ sauce
2 Tablespoons water
¼ cup milk
1 egg
1 can Pringles

Instructions:

1. Preheat oven to 400 degrees.
2. Cut chicken breasts into strips.
3. Mix BBQ sauce, water, egg, and milk in shallow dish.
4. Lay strips of chicken in dish and make sure they are all covered with the mixture. Refrigerate until ready to cook.
5. Crush Pringles and roll the chicken strips into the chips to cover them. Place on baking sheet. Bake 10 minutes, flip over, and then bake for another 3–5 minutes.

COST
Per Recipe: **$5.49**
Per Serving: **$1.37 [Restaurant Price: $9.95]**

---

* ***ANNUAL SAVINGS*: *$983***

2. Baked Lemon Chicken (Ready in 35 minutes; Makes 5)

3 ½ pounds chicken, skinned and cut into 10 pieces
¼ teaspoon salt
¼ teaspoon pepper
1 teaspoon garlic powder
3 cups thinly sliced onions
1 ½ cups chicken stock or water
¼ cup lemon juice
1 lemon sliced into 10 slices, seeds removed

Instructions:

1. Combine salt, pepper, garlic, and thyme.
2. Lay chicken pieces into an 11x13 baking pan. Sprinkle seasonings over chicken.
3. Combine onions, stock, and lemon juice in a sauce pan. Heat to a boil.
4. Pour hot lemon mixture around chicken. Top each chicken piece with a lemon slice.
5. Bake for 30 minutes at 400 degrees until golden brown and juices are clear colored.

COST
Per Recipe: **$ 4.90**
Per Serving: **$ 0.98 [Restaurant Price: 14.99]**

3. Italian Broccoli and Pasta (Ready in 25 minutes; Makes 4)

2 cups fettuccini noodles, uncooked
3 Tablespoons chopped green onion (also called scallions)
2 cups broccoli florets
½ teaspoon dried thyme
½ teaspoon dried oregano
½ teaspoon black pepper
1 can (14.5 ounces) stewed tomatoes
2 teaspoons grated Parmesan cheese

Instructions:

1. Cook noodles according to package instructions (do not include oil or salt), and drain.
2. Spray a medium skillet with nonstick cooking spray; stir-fry onion and broccoli for 3 minutes over medium heat.
3. Add seasonings (but not the Parmesan cheese) and tomatoes; simmer until heated through.
4. Spoon vegetable mixture over noodles and top with Parmesan cheese.

COST
Per Recipe: **$3.13**
Per Serving: **$0.78 [Restaurant Price: $12.99]**

4. Roasted Herb Potatoes (Ready in 35 minutes; Makes 6) [VEGETARIAN!]

Vegetable cooking spray
1 pound (3 medium or 3 cups cubed) potatoes
2 teaspoons vegetable-oil
½ teaspoon rosemary
½ teaspoon salt

Instructions:

1. Preheat the oven to 450 degrees.
2. Coat a baking sheet with vegetable cooking spray.
3. Wash and peel the potatoes.
4. Cut the potatoes into ½-inch cubes, and put them in a large bowl.
5. Put the oil, rosemary, and salt in a small bowl. Stir together.
6. Pour the oil mix over the potatoes. Stir to coat the potatoes evenly.
7. Spread the potatoes on the baking sheet.
8. Bake for 25 to 30 minutes, or until lightly browned.

COST
Per Recipe: **$0.94**
Per Serving: **$0.16 [Restaurant Price: $8.99]**

5. Quick Chili (Ready in 20 minutes; Makes 4)

½ pound ground beef
1 can (15.5 ounces) kidney beans with liquid
1 cup tomato sauce, no salt added
1 Tablespoon onion, instant minced
1 ½ Tablespoons chili powder

Instructions:

1. Thoroughly cook ground beef in skillet until browned. Be sure all pink color is gone from meat and juices.
2. Drain off fat into container.
3. Stir in kidney beans with liquid, tomato sauce, onion, and chili powder.
4. Bring to a boil. Reduce heat, cover, and simmer for 10 minutes.
5. Refrigerate or freeze leftovers within 2 hours of cooking. Use refrigerated leftovers within 4 days.

COST
Per Recipe: **$2.80**
Per Serving: **$0.70 [Restaurant Price: $6.49]**

6. Tortilla Pizzas (Ready in 25 minutes; Makes 6) [VEGETARIAN!]

12 small flour or corn tortillas
Vegetable oil or margarine
1 can (16 ounces) refried beans
¼ cup chopped onion
2 ounces diced fresh or canned green chili peppers
6 Tablespoons red taco sauce
3 cups chopped vegetables, such as broccoli, mushrooms, spinach, and red bell peppers
½ cup cheese, shredded part-skim mozzarella
½ cup chopped, fresh cilantro

Instructions:

1. Brush one side of each of two tortillas with water. Press the wet sides of the tortillas together to form a thick crust for the pizza.
2. Brush the outside of the tortillas with a small amount of oil or margarine. Evenly brown both sides in a heated frying pan. Repeat with the rest of the tortillas. Set aside.
3. Heat refried beans, onion, and half of the chili peppers together in a medium saucepan, stirring occasionally. Remove from heat.
4. Spread about 1/3 cup of the bean mixture on each tortilla pizza. Sprinkle with 1 Tablespoon taco sauce, then top with ½ cup of the chopped vegetables, 1 teaspoon chili peppers, and 1 Tablespoon cheese for each pizza.
5. Return to frying pan and heat until cheese melts. Top with cilantro, if desired. Serve immediately.

COST
Per Recipe: **$3.75**
Per Serving: **$0.62 [Restaurant Price: $5.99]**

7. Quick Beef and Rice (Ready in 25 minutes; Makes 6)

1 pound ground beef or turkey
2 cups rice
1 package onion soup mix
4 cups water
1 can (15-ounce) cream of mushroom soup

Instructions:

1. Brown the ground meat and drain if necessary.
2. Add soup mix, rice, soup, and water and bring to a boil.
3. Cover and simmer for 20 minutes, until rice is done.

COST
Per Recipe: **$7.40**
Per Serving: **$1.23 [Restaurant Price: $9.99]**

8. Chicken and Veggies Stir Fry (Ready in 25 minutes; Makes 6)

1 package of boneless chicken breasts
¼ bag of frozen stir-fry vegetables
1 Tablespoon of vegetable oil
Rice, white or brown

Instructions:

1. Begin cooking rice, per package directions (should take less than 20 minutes).
2. Rinse chicken and cut into bite-size pieces. Brown in a nonstick skillet, over medium-high heat, until cooked well.
3. Add cooked chicken into veggies and simmer 5 minutes to blend well, stirring occasionally.
4. Remove chicken and veggies from pan and serve over warm rice.

COST
Per Recipe: **$7.96**
Per Serving: **$1.33 [Restaurant Price: $11.99]**

TOTAL ANNUAL SAVINGS: $2,175

ONLINE RESOURCES

Check out the USDA's Recipe Finder Database at recipefinder.nal.usda.gov. This is a well-designed site with hundreds of recipes that allows you to search by preparation time, recipe costs, cooking equipment, nutritional value and ingredients. Each recipe comes with a per serving and per recipe price tag as well as a "Nutrition Facts" label that lets you know exactly how many calories and grams of fat you'll be cooking up. There's also an "add to shopping list" feature that automatically combines all of the ingredients you will need to purchase in order to make the recipes of your choice. It's ".gov" so you don't have to fight off any pesky ads—browse in peace.

OTHER GREAT SITES FOR SIMPLE, BUDGET-FRIENDLY MEALS WITH SHORT PREP TIMES

1. **Allrecipes.com.** Plug in the ingredients you've found on sale and receive a personalized recipe. They also have a free iPhone app.
2. **Yumyum.com/student.** In addition to tons of recipes, YumYum has great "beginner's" information for the iLifer living on his or her own for the first time.
3. **Recipezaar.com.** Check out the "College Budget Recipes" cookbook.
4. **Cheaprecipes.org.**
5. **Startcooking.com.**

CHAPTER 11

ENTERTAINMENT.

"As a share of Gross Domestic Product (GDP), consumer spending on what might reasonably be called 'pop culture' held roughly stable at around 3 percent of GDP from the late 1920s until the early 1980s, or over half a century. Thereafter, it rose dramatically, from 3.4 percent of GDP ($71 billion) in 1982 to 5.4 percent of GDP ($361 billion) in 2000. The entire Millennial childhood has coincided with an explosive entertainment spending boom fueled by their (Boomer and Gen-X) parents and older siblings."

—WILLIAM STRAUSS AND NEIL HOWE,
MILLENNIALS AND THE POP CULTURE (2006)

SPENDING BREAKDOWN

iLIFER: STAN D'ARD

CURRENT: Pre-$15,000-Year Expenditures
ANNUAL: $2,472
MONTHLY: $206

TARGET: $15,000 Year Expenditures
ANNUAL: $1,008
MONTHLY: $85

SAVINGS: **$1,464**

The recent rise in young adult entertainment spending makes it clear that iLifers like to have fun and don't particularly mind shelling out large chunks of cash for TV, movies, partying, sports and travel. The good news for the $15K-Yearer is that most of these leisure activities can be experienced for free or for only a few bucks. This chapter takes on the sacred cow of entertainment spending and shows you how to have fun without sacrificing your financial security this year . Here's a breakdown of what you'll see in the following pages.

- **Movies**
- **7 Reasons to Go Cable-Free**
- **Reading**
- **(Other) Cheap Thrills**
- **Talk is Cheap: Cell Phone Services**

MOVIES

A 2007 survey by Harris Interactive found that college students over-index on movie ticket purchases, spending an average of $70 per year to see movies, compared to just $32 for the general population. Add the $7 worth of snacks that the average moviegoer buys and the occasional $1.50 "convenience" charge for online ticket purchases, and the typical iLifer is spending almost $150 per year at the movie theater. Movies are a relatively cheap form of entertainment, but you can add another 100 bucks towards your $15,000 savings by making a few minor changes in this area:

Theater Hop*.

Picnic It. Food and drink prices are super-inflated at theaters and the popcorn bar is no place for the $15K-Yearer. I'm serious. Remember that there's a recession going on and stuff your pockets (or your oversized celebrity purse) with goodies from your pantry or even make a pit stop at a corner store on your way to the Cineplex.

ANNUAL SAVINGS: ***$55***

iMax-ed Out My Credit Card to Come Here. See more. Hear more. Feel more. Pay more. The iMax Experience. So I hear iMax theatres are worth the extra three or four bucks (or, 30–40 *percent*). I'll have to get back to you on that. For now, if only to test your level of restraint and commitment this year, stick with the "regular" movie theaters that were just fine before you knew what an iMax was.

ANNUAL SAVINGS: $25

Wait a While. Some cities have reduced-price theaters that show movies a few weeks after they've debuted in the first-run theaters. Have a little patience and watch the flick when it's $2, not $12.

ANNUAL SAVINGS: $49

Previews and Reviews. The only thing worse than losing two hours of your life watching a bad movie is the fact that you lost $11.75. Embark on a three-step vetting process before you spend a dime at the cinema. First, read a couple reviews online by film critics you trust. Second, put the movie you're interested in to a Youtube test. Watch the official preview and a couple extra clips on Youtube or Apple.com to see if the storyline, humor, cinematography and acting are up to par. Finally, get word-of-mouth endorsements from friends with similar tastes. The last

*www.wikihow.com/Theater-Hop

step—the most important of the three—means that you won't be able to see the movie on its release day. But you'll be doing yourself a favor by avoiding the crowds and the flashing red "SOLD-OUT" sign blues. Give your Facebook friends the privilege of going through all that and then find out if the movie was really worth it. Watch out for spoilers...

ANNUAL SAVINGS: $32

Free Screenings! Register at sites like www.filmmetro.com and www.thescreeningexchange.com to get free tickets to never-before-seen movies in your city. Or head back to school. Colleges often host free screenings of unreleased and recently released films. Dust off your old sweatshirt from your alma mater and drive over to campus for a free flick with a little nostalgia on the side. Libraries, city parks and museums also offer free film nights, although the movies are rarely new.

Watch Online. There are hundreds of websites that allow you to watch recently released films on your laptop for free. I could list some of them here, but chances are they'll be shut down by the powers that be and replaced by 10 others by the time you read this.

ANNUAL SAVINGS: $45

Netflix for Your Net Worth. Twelve bucks a month for rentals is a little steep but if you watch a lot of movies, it's worth it. You can also use Netflix to watch movies and TV shows online without waiting for shipping.

ANNUAL SAVINGS: $41
(Up to $133 for movie lovers.)

Redbox. Wal-Mart and a few other stores have $1 per night rental vending machines that allow you to pick up movies and return them to any portal in your area. Find locations in your area by putting in your ZIP code at www.redbox.com.

TV

THE $15,000 YEAR ENDORSES... Kicking Cable to the Curb... and cozying up to any of its more advanced, more interactive and, most importantly, more cost-effective successors. Join the Movement.

With cable prices on the rise and TV-on-the-Web becoming more accessible, a growing number of watchers have decided to save hundreds of dollars annually by simply cancelling their cable subscriptions.

This is a great way for the $15,000 Year participant to cut out up to $1,000 from his or her annual costs without sacrificing much. Most iLifers already know how to access their favorite shows online but many are reluctant to fully desert cable, choosing instead to use their laptops as a supplement to traditional television. Hopefully, the following pages will convince you to go *sans*-cable for the year and get your TV without paying for it.

7 Reasons to Go Cable-Free This Year

1. **Costs.** Cable TV prices have risen more than 75 percent since 1996, according to the BLS. Depending on which statistics you look at, the average monthly cable bill in the U.S. is somewhere between $60 and $99. Most subscribers are essentially giving a lot of this money away to their cable company because the average American only watches about 15 of the 118 available channels. Cable companies have basically laughed in the face of the idea that customers should be able to pay for only the channels they want. In addition to rising and hidden costs, this inflexibility is one of the reasons Cable TV received a last place trophy from the American Consumer Satisfaction Index survey in 2005.

2. **We Interrupt These Commercials To Bring You Actual Programming.** While we could spend hours debating whether the quality of TV programming has declined or improved during the past 15 years, one indisputable fact is that there has been a decline in *quantity*. Obviously I don't mean the number of shows. I'm talking about the content-to-commercials ratio. According to a 2003 study, the big four TV networks aired an average of 52 minutes of noncontent* during the prime time period of 8 to 11 p.m., an increase of 36 percent since 1991. More recent reports by Nielsen show continued increases in commercials during daytime and primetime hours, leaving viewers with more ads and less show. FYI, the average American will spend nearly two years watching television commercials over a lifetime.

3. **Product Placement.** Many TV show sets have become walking commercials as product placement has proliferated on reality shows, sitcoms and dramas during the last 10 years. According

*A total of 130 commercials, promos and PSAs.

to the 2006 TNS Media Intelligence study, the average primetime show contains four minutes and 25 seconds of product placement. When Tyra gives her protégés makeovers on *America's Next Top Model*, it's important that viewers hear the promotional slogan for the new CoverGirl LashBlast Luxe mascara*. When Simon and Co. are evaluating *Idol* contestants, they must constantly sip from logoed-out cups of Coca-Cola. Jack Bauer and Dexter have to hot-wire the cars and bug the cell phones made by the companies that have climbed into bed with *Fox* and *Showtime*. Product placement is annoying, you can't TiVo through it and it often disrupts the continuity (or the authenticity) of TV shows.

4. **Better Things to Do.** The average American spends 1,306.6 hours annually, or 43.2 days, watching TV. This is 39 percent higher than the total in 1960 and translates into billions of dollars worth of lost productivity and millions of pounds of gained weight. Deloitte's 2008 State of the Media Democracy survey found that iLifers spend one-third less time watching TV than other generations†. You won't miss reality TV if you're too busy enjoying reality (see "Cheap Thrills" section below).
5. **Looking Forward.** Techno-heads are working diligently to make the Internet-TV experience as pleasant as possible by improving video quality and eliminating malfunctions. Soon, there will be an affordable, seamless process for streaming your shows onto your television set in a way that leaves your laptop available for Skyping, blogging and surfing while you watch. And by affordable, I mean free.
6. **P2P.** It's likely that you are already a pro at using the Internet to watch your favorite shows, clips and movies and any advice I give you will probably be out of date by the time this book reaches your possession. But that's a good thing. We live in a world where techno-libertarians are constantly coming up with new ways to share content with others, without playing by the rules of the big monopolists that have traditionally controlled entertainment channels with an iron fist. Because of democratizing platforms like Youtube, much of the most entertaining, engaging and authentic video content can't be found on cable TV. It's being created and

---

* "Big, bold lashes, now with a hint of shimmer!"

† The survey also found that three-quarters of iLifers view their computer as more entertaining than their television.

virally marketed by regular people all over the country who don't ask for money and who are often more creative and original than the execs calling the shots at major media corporations.

7. **DTV.** The 2009 conversion to all-digital television broadcasting has created more free programming. There's actually some pretty good stuff on PBS—and it's commercial free.

TOTAL ANNUAL SAVINGS: **$925**

NOTE: Lose the cable, but keep the TV. Watching local programming or rented movies and DVD series is a good way to make sure your TV set doesn't feel neglected when you break up with cable. Also, TV set prices have fallen by 75 percent since 2000.

READING

I may be cutting my career as a writer short by saying this but, here goes: you should rarely, if ever, spend any money on books.

I'm definitely not saying that you shouldn't read. In fact, you could save a lot of money by reading more. Reading is one of the cheapest leisure activities and the modern marketplace is full of options for free access to literature.

THE $15,000 YEAR ENDORSES... The Library.

Head over to the library. Public libraries have done a good job of staying current and embracing technology to improve their services. And people have reacted. Visits to public libraries in the US increased 61 percent between 1994 and 2004, according to *Book Trends: 2007*. And the recession has only accelerated this increase. The *Wall Street Journal* reported jumps in public library patronage of up to 65 percent between 2007 and 2008.

Libraries offer access to a wide range of free resources including movies, CDs, magazines and, naturally, books. With efficient interlibrary loaning systems, you can submit an online request for a title that's not available at your local library and they'll often have it shipped over from a different branch (they may even purchase a new copy for you). If you need to hold onto your book for another two weeks, you can usually renew the book online in less than a minute (after receiving a courtesy due date notice via email).

> *"Libraries are the ultimate resource for anyone who wants it all but doesn't want to spend anything to get it. After all, the libraries were established by Mr. 'A Penny Saved is a Penny Earned' himself, Benjamin Franklin."*
>
> —ROB GRADER, *The Cheap Bastard's Guide to New York City* (2008)

Libraries (and bookstores) can be great entertainment spots when you're low on cash. Many offer free Wi-Fi and access to the latest magazines. You can strike up conversations with staff or strangers or just enjoy the smell of coffee and new books. The Santa Monica Public Library, which is sort of like a Barnes & Nobles, Blockbuster and Apple Store all wrapped into one, houses thousands of books, new release DVDs, CDs, video games, computers, hotspots and new magazines—and everything is free! It has video tutorials, a Web 2.0 catalog system and even a Facebook page. I'm a fan…

Find the best library in your area, sign up for a card and become a regular there.

ANNUAL SAVINGS: $391

OTHER READING

Free Books! Head to www.bookcrossing.com (aka, the world's biggest free book club). More than 750,000 people in 130 countries use this site to share their love of books by leaving them for others to pick up on park benches, in coffee shops or at vacation hotels. It's a uniquely 21st century model that's socially responsible and wallet-friendly. Register with the site and pick up books left in your neighborhood—or drop one off and track it online to see where in the world it ends up.

eBook it. These are apparently the books of the future and companies like Google are leading the digitization race of the new millennium. Google provides free previews of books that can run longer than 100 pages. It's entirely possible to get all the information you need from a book by reading through one of these extended previews. (About 10 percent of the research for this book was conducted via eBooks and Google's Book Search.)

Re: Kindle. Amazon released the Kindle 2.0 device in 2009, furthering its attempt to revolutionize the world of the written word. If you already have one, great. If you don't, wait—for two inevitable events to occur before you purchase it:

1. The price of the device to go down (should be under $150 in the near future).

2. Some college whiz kid to trigger a new round of intellectual property hearings by creating free software that allows readers to download or share digital books with others free of charge.

Magazines. Paying the $4 cover price for a magazine at the grocery store or the airport is madness. Check out sites like www.BestDealMagazines.com to find super-cheap one-year magazine subscriptions for less than a fiver. If you're a real magazine-head, start a magazine co-op with some of your friends or neighbors and share subscriptions, rotating each issue.

TOTAL ANNUAL SAVINGS: ***$102***

Cheap Thrills

From vacationing to partying, here are a few more ways to save cash on entertainment.

Staycation. Skip your vacation this year and do a "staycation" while you pay off your credit card debt. Once you are debt free (and have saved yourself thousands by avoiding years of interest payments), take yourself to Europe or St. Kitts for a celebration.

SAVINGS: ***$642***

Staycation (2.0). You are now free to move about the city. Spend this year's vacation enjoying the treasures of the city you live in. Many people spend years living in a locale and never see any of the gems that the city is famous for. Cram all of your domestic tourism into one week and call it a vacation.

ANNUAL SAVINGS: **$539**

You Need to Get *Out* More. The great American outdoors, that is. Camping, hiking, fishing, canoeing and other forms of recreation that your "wired" kids will look at you funny for even suggesting—they're all free or low-cost.

If You Must... If you're dead set on jet setting out of the country this year, try to do it on the cheap. Stretch your money by going where the dollar is strong. Sleep in budget hotels or stay with friends and distant acquaintances. Avoid tourist traps. Go to the library and check out a copy of "*Let's Go:* [insert destination] *on a Budget*" or a comparable budget travel guide. These books usually pay for themselves so they are worth the $15 cover price if you can't find a free copy.

ANNUAL SAVINGS: ***$137***

Life's a Beach. Free tanning available! If you live near the ocean (or any body of water), take advantage of this low-cost leisure activity.

Not Your Mother's Museum. Today's art, history and science museums often bring a 21st century flair to classic collections. Stats show that iLifers are 44 percent more likely to go to museums than young people of the 1970s. Although admission to popular museums can often cost more than a movie ticket, it's relatively easy to see timeless art without spending a dime. Many smaller museums are completely free and the major ones tend to have free or "pay-what-you-wish" days every month. Check the museum's website to find out when you can visit for free*.

Theater. Try to find free theater productions in your community. Colleges, community centers and churches often have free or low-price shows. If you're itching to see a pricey performance, call the theater to see if you can volunteer as an usher and watch the show for free. In bigger cities, sites such as Goldstar.com, Going.com and Yelp.com list discounted or free events.

Music Performances. Pretend to be an A&R and hit the underground circuit for performances by up-and-coming artists. Before she became a Grammy winner, Norah Jones could be seen doing free gigs at The Living Room in lower Manhattan. Since most up-and-coming musicians have free music available online, you can hear a sample of their work before deciding whether or not to venture out and hear them live. Five years from now, you'll be able to say you knew them back when.

> NOTE: Beware of drink minimums at some of these "free" shows. If you spend $20 on two drinks at a free performance, you just paid $14 for your ticket without realizing it.

Free Laughs. Laugh all the way to the bank by finding free stand-up comedy and improv shows in your city. You may get what you pay for, but, in the age of *awkward,* "not funny" can be hilarious in its own weird way.

Sports and Rec. Kill two birds with one stone: entertain yourself and get your exercise by playing free sports—pickup basketball, running, biking, softball, beach volleyball, etc. Most communities and many workplaces have organized programs for these and other sports. Or,

---

*A large number of museums have been hit especially hard by the recession. If you can afford it, toss a couple bucks in the pay-what-you-wish bucket as you leave.

you can always just head over to your local park or community center to play along.

> NOTE: If you're a big sports fan, attending college and pro sports games can set you back hundreds of dollars. Check Craigslist for cheap tickets or try to find a college student who will sell you his or her reduced price seat. You'll fit in just fine in the student section.

Game Night. Instead of going out with your friends to a pricey restaurant where you have to keep your voice down, host a game night in your apartment and let loose. Have your friends bring over their favorite games, or use the 18 bucks you would've spent on a forgettable meal and buy a copy of the timeless instigator of good times, *Taboo.*

Go Out. But Stay In. An intriguing concept explained in the blogosphere by my good friend Miss Moneypenny*:

Go Out At Home

Posted on Thursday, February 19, 2009 at 09:03PM

> I love this one—I'd do it even if the economy wasn't in the crapper. Going out to clubs has got to be one of the biggest expenses of the young and social (like yourselves).... You end up standing the cold for 30 minutes because you got the club early enough to get in free, only to find out the bouncer isn't letting anyone in for less than $20. THEN, once you are inside (feet aching and fingers numb), all the guys are too broke to actually buy you a drink, which in turn, depresses you enough that you break down and whip out the debt card just to take yourself out of your own misery. Finally, as the night winds down, you have to remember to get cash for the valet (because street parking is an invitation to get stalked by drunk, homeless men). All said, you're probably going home alone and $50 dollars poorer. Why was this a good idea???
>
> So, what to do with your Friday nights? Go out at home. As my friends will attest, I love this strategy. I do it pretty much every weekend. Invite a bunch of people over and tell everyone to bring a stranger and a drink. You get to meet new fun people, have a few laughs, and save a lot of money. Just invest in a few good bottles of [*$15K Year censorship*: water], have a few board games on hand, have a good playlist, and the party is on! Because, really, are you actually going to meet your future husband in the club?"

---

*missmoneypenny.squarespace.com

Get on Mailing Lists. Here's another instance where having that second or third email account comes into play. Sign up for as many online newsletters as you please and receive insider information about performances, concerts and comedy shows.

DOG DAYS

How much is that doggy in the window? According to the ASPCA, $780 per year in upkeep costs (and possibly hundreds more to buy). Postpone that pet purchase for a year and you'll be able to pamper your poodle. If you're itching for non-human companionship, a goldfish costs less than $25 a year to maintain.

Benefits. Find out if your company has partnerships with any other organizations that will give you free or reduced price admission to museums, movies, concerts and sporting events.

Craigslist. Kill time at work by checking Craigslist for free and dirt cheap tickets being sold by people who can no longer attend an event.

*TOTAL ANNUAL SAVINGS: **$791+***

Talk is Cheap: Cell Phone Services

In 2007, spending on cell phone services surpassed landline expenditures for the first time in history and I doubt America will ever look back. Unsurprisingly, young people led the way in this category, directing 75 percent of telephone expenditures to cell phones, according to the BLS. Based on stats like this, I probably don't need to tell you to take an anti-landline approach during the $15,000 Year (*ANNUAL SAVINGS: **$338***).

But, even if you're already using your cell phone exclusively, don't think you're "off the hook" (sorry, couldn't resist). You probably would do your bank account a favor by taking a good look at your phone bill and your usage patterns and making some adjustments.

The average under-25 consumer unit spends $744 per year on cell phone services. For college grads with steady incomes, you should bump that number up 31 percent to about $975, or $81 per month. This number leaves a lot of room for cost cutting and the following tips will help you pocket an extra $300 or more this year.

Even if you're locked into an expensive data plan for your PDA or iPhone, you should consider reducing your minutes and switching to a plan that's more $15K-Year friendly. Visit www.BillShrink.com. Fill out a quick five-question form, telling the folks at BillShrink how much you're currently paying and how much you normally talk and text (or just import your most recent cell phone bill) and they'll tell you which service plans are best for you and which carriers will offer you decent rates and a strong signal (based on your zip code). This free service gets the $15,000 Year seal of approval because it lets you know exactly how much you'd be saving per year by making the advised switch.

But BillShrink should be just a starting point. For those who are paying for more cell service than they use, it's a good way to help you stop giving away free money to the phone companies. For everyone else, achieving significant savings on cell phone services will require a few lifestyle changes. Now, I realize that we love our phones and prefer to cut back in every other area rather than sacrifice our technology to the budgeting gods so I'll try to make this as painless as possible.

The good news is that the next wave of communication is slowly replacing the traditional mobile phone model and 21st century alternatives provide more options for free connectivity than ever before.

(Don't) Put Your Money Where Your Mouth Is: Tips for saving hundreds on your cell phone bill

First: Monitor Your Usage. It's extremely simple and extremely important to check your usage balance regularly. You can do this online or by dialing up a free text message from your carrier with usage information (See box below for numbers and instructions).

Here's a surefire way to remind yourself to do this: Put the book down and pull out your cell phone. Set a recurring monthly reminder on your phone's calendar that will alert you on the 15th and 25th of every month to send for this text and check up on your minutes.

This is the most important step because the successful completion of the $15K Year relies on you avoiding major fiscal blunders and mistakes, especially preventable ones. Trust me, there will be enough unexpected financial setbacks that threaten to derail you—no need for self-inflicted wounds.

If the "I-went-way-over-my-monthly-minutes-allowance-oh-my-Lord-look-at-this-bill" blues have never happened to you, you've

CHECKING YOUR USAGE

- **VERIZON WIRELESS** customers can check their minutes used by dialing **#MIN (or, #646).** Verizon will send you a free text with your information. To check your account balance, call **#BAL (or, #225)**.
- **AT&T** customers can check their balance by calling ***646#.** AT&T will send a text message with remaining minutes available.
- **SPRINT NEXTEL** subscribers: Dial ***4** to check your both your minutes used and account balance.
- **T-MOBILE** customers can get balance, usage and messaging information. To track minutes used, call **#MIN# (or, #646#)**. For messages used, call **#MSG# (or, #674#)**. Dialing **#BAL# (or, #225#)** and pressing send will get you your balance.

NOTE: Use these reports only as estimates, as they usually don't include calls made in the last 24 hours.

probably had a friend who used up her anytime minutes and continued to chat away even as her carrier charged oppressive rates of up to $0.49 per minute. She may have come to you in tears with a $573 phone bill after getting icy treatment from an insensitive customer service rep who insisted that she pay the full amount or have her phone line and her credit wiped out. The phone companies make a lot of money from people like this so make sure you keep an eye on your monthly minutes balance. (While the $15K Year generally doesn't endorse spending *more* money on anything, it's a wise decision to upgrade for more minutes if you find yourself consistently using more than your allotted anytime time—but try some of the options below first.)

ANNUAL SAVINGS: ***UP TO $573***

Free Nights and Weekends. Use your work phone for daytime calls or simply send an email. If someone calls you at 8:55 pm and you talk for an hour, you just gave away 55 of your anytime minutes to the your service provider (I doubt they say "Thank you"). Once the clock strikes 9 pm*, hang up and call back for free.

ANNUAL SAVINGS: ***UP TO $180***

---

*Consider paying a little extra for early nights and weekends if you do most of your talking in the late evening. With AT&T, it'll cost you about $120 over the course of a year to upgrade to free calls after 7 p.m.

Love Don't Cost a Thing. Before you engage in a two-hour flirt session with your fiancée-to-be on a weekday, make sure the person you're coquetting with is on the same network and qualifies for free mobile-to-mobile (if he really loves you, he'll switch over to your carrier). Otherwise, head over to Skype or G-Chat or call them back during night or weekend minutes.

Free Speech Movement. There are plenty of cost-free ways to keep in touch with your friends and loved ones, with Skype* and Gmail Video Chat being two popular ones. Cutting back on your costly cell phone minutes and replacing your phone time with any of these 21st century platforms for free communication could save you hundreds.

ANNUAL SAVINGS: $359

PAYGers. If you're a light talker (or a super Skyper), consider a pay-as-you-go setup that gives you the convenience of a cell phone without the monthly bill. These are typically ideal for people who use their phones for an average of less than 350 minutes a month (about 12 minutes per day) and don't text too often. Already the standard model in Europe, Asia and Africa, pay-as-you-go is gaining popularity in the U.S., where sales grew three times faster than traditional cell phone plans in 2008, according to Pali Research. Prepaid carriers now offer a lot more flexibility than they have in the past and, perhaps their best feature, they don't lock you in a 24-month jail-like cell contract.

ANNUAL SAVINGS: $390+
(It may be worth the $175 termination fee to get out of your costly mobile phone plan before your contract runs out.)

Check Please! Look at Your Bill. Cell phone companies are singular in their ability to nickel and dime extra fees and costs onto a bill (one of the reasons *Consumer Reports* rated the industry near the bottom of the customer satisfaction hierarchy in 2007). Make sure you're not being charged for anything you didn't sign up for and definitely give the customer service department an earful if you catch your carrier trying to pull one over. (It's usually a free call.)

> *"Since January 2002, wireless providers have charged customers nearly $1 billion in additional fees that have all kinds of nebulous*

---

*Skype is a software application that allows users to make free telephone calls over the Internet. It recently released an iPhone App, allowing iPhone users to call other Skypers without using any cell phone minutes (www.skype.com).

names like the 'Federal Programs Cost Recovery Fee,' and other various and sundry surcharges, taxes and fees. Let's get real. Those costs were never disclosed to you when you signed the contract. They appeared only after you signed your life away for at least a year. Probably two."

—MARY HUNT for Everyday Cheapskate Newsletter, *Hunting for Hidden Fees*, January 26, 2009

Smart Spending. If you have a smart phone, make sure to legitimize its high costs by taking advantage of its features, many of which can save you money in other areas. Use your phone as the GPS system for your car (*SAVINGS: $109*). Download applications with VoIP to make free local calls and cheap international calls* (*ANNUAL SAVINGS: $62*). Use free eBook apps to download free classics† (*ANNUAL SAVINGS:* $22). Look up the cheapest gas station between your job and your apartment while you commute‡ (*ANNUAL SAVINGS: $57*). Other apps and services will help you find recipes and low-cost restaurants, allow you to do consumer product research and price comparisons while you're in the store and even help you avoid speeding tickets by alerting you to common speed traps§.

ANNUAL SAVINGS: $298

Good Textiquette. Texting is a novel form of communication but, with overage rates of up to $0.25 per msg, it can be downright dangerous if you use it too often. Unless you have an unlimited texting plan, don't waste 30 texts trying to decide which movie to see with your friends. This debate could easily be settled with a couple 30-second phone calls (or by email). Check out websites like www.onlinetextmessage.com, which allows you to send free texts from your laptop or send an email to the email-to-SMS gateway for the recipient's carrier (e.g., 9175551234@vtext.com to text a Verizon customer).

ANNUAL SAVINGS: $19

When in Roam... Money-hungry mobile phone companies salivate when you leave the country or step outside their traditional coverage area. If you make a call, send a text or access the Web from Canada, Cancun or the Caribbean, be prepared to pay up to $4 per minute. Yes,

---

*iPhone App: Cheap International

†iPhone App: eReader

‡iPhone App: iGasUp

§iPhone Apps: BigOven, Amazon Mobile and SpeedTrap, respectively

per minute. Carriers rarely advertise these exorbitant rates so if you're unsure of what you'll be charged, simply turn your phone off until you're back in the land of the free nights and weekends.

ANNUAL SAVINGS: UP TO $140

> *"Cell-phone service seems to stubbornly resist improvement. The Annual Survey of Cell-Phone Service conducted by the Consumer Reports National Research Center found that fewer than half of respondents were completely or very satisfied. That makes cell service among the lower-rated services we survey, as it has been for the past six years."*
>
> —CONSUMER REPORTS, January 15, 2008

Employee Discounts. Thousands of companies, organizations and universities have agreements with mobile phone carriers. Check to see if any of your affiliations can help you slash 15 percent or more from your monthly bill.

ANNUAL SAVINGS: $144

LIVE AND DIRECT

Before you make a customer service call, visit www.gethuman.com to make sure you don't waste five to 10 anytime minutes listening to recorded messages. This website has a database of more than 500 companies and will tell you exactly what number combinations to dial in order to bypass automated phone systems and talk to a live person who can answer your questions quickly. For example, if you need to speak to a customer service rep at Expedia, press "0#" at each prompt, ignoring the messages.

CHAPTER 12

APPAREL & APPEARANCE.

"Judging from the styles on display at [the 2009 New York] fashion week, a recession does wonders for creativity."

—CHRISTINA BINKLEY FOR THE WALL STREET JOURNAL
LEAN TIMES BEGET FRESH FASHION IDEAS
FEBRUARY 18, 2009

SPENDING BREAKDOWN

iLIFER: STAN D'ARD

CURRENT: Pre-$15,000-Year Expenditures
ANNUAL: $2,056
MONTHLY: $171

TARGET: $15,000 Year Expenditures
ANNUAL: $960
MONTHLY: $80

SAVINGS: **$1,096**

Now that it's chic to be cheap, it's officially safe for all you thrifty fashionistas to come out of your half-priced closets and proclaim your frugality to the world. Flaunt your designer knockoffs and dirt-cheap accessories with confidence. Pop your "slightly irregular" collar with pride. When someone compliments you on that dress you bought for 85 percent off at TJ Maxx, never again pretend like you don't remember where you got it or how much you paid for it. Take pride in your thrift and continue to create the looks of the season at a fraction of retail. Now's your time in the spotlight and, all of a sudden, all the cool kids want to be like you. Enjoy it while it lasts.

Unfortunately, market research has consistently found that most young people don't fit the above description—and actually tend to be more likely than any other age group to overspend on fashion. Our standard iLifer forks over more than $2,000 a year for apparel—regularly buying evanescent threads on impulse and on credit.

The 2007 Simmons National Consumer Survey found 18- to 24-year-olds were twice as likely as older adults to agree with the statement "I spend more than I can afford on clothes." We are also the most likely to discard clothes that are less than a year old and to head to the mall even if we don't need anything.

iLIFERS ON APPAREL			
	18–24	25–34	34+
I make my clothes last a long time.	69%	76%	78%
I dress to please myself.	69%	73%	77%
I stick with styles that have stood the test of time.	47%	58%	64%
Function is the most important factor in clothes I buy.	43%	54%	59%
I like to keep up with the latest fashion.	38%	31%	25%
I like to experiment with new styles.	41%	29%	23%
Top designers make quality clothes.	32%	26%	24%
I often buy clothes I don't really need.	31%	22%	22%
I like to make a unique fashion statement.	31%	19%	16%
Every season I buy the latest fashions.	23%	16%	12%
I no longer wear clothes I wore a year ago.	21%	14%	12%
I am first among my friends to try new styles.	22%	14%	10%

Source: National Consumer Survey, Simmons NCS (2007)

These statistics, coupled with the fact that young people direct a larger percentage of their incomes towards clothing than any other age group, are pretty clear indicators that good old fashion consumerism is alive and well for iLifers in the 21st century. But, thankfully, this data was taken before the 2008 recession smacked the rose-colored shopper shades off our faces. For most iLifers—along with just about every other cohort of consumers—the economic downturn has clipped our Vicky Secrets angels' wings and dropped us humbly back into the realm of reality. Or, at least Ross.

But the beautiful thing about this reality is that young people, loaded with creativity and flexibility, are learning to build expressive and fashion-conscious wardrobes without breaking bank. Much to the chagrin of the designer apparel industry, the 2008 recession exposed a long-closeted secret: Saving money on clothes can be done without sacrificing style. In fact, it's entirely possible that you'll become *more* stylish by adopting a more economical approach.

That's what this chapter is about.

Apparel

After doing a little background research on the fashion industry, I discovered how much of a premium fashion retailers charge shoppers for designer apparel. The numbers are shocking. Clothes-makers may boast about the level of detail and attention they put into designing each garment, but the truth is that most apparel is extremely cheap to produce and distribute. That Bebe top was made by the same underpaid factory workers who manufactured the similar shirt at JC Penney, or even K-Mart. The Bebe consumer pays $39.99 for the "Tab Shoulder Blouson Metallic Top" and the JCP shopper pays $16.99 for the "Squareneck Bow Top", but each shirt cost the apparel makers something like $5 for the material and labor.

The largest supply-side cost differences are usually related to the number of marketing dollars spent to promote the more expensive labels. The fashion industry spends billions of dollars per year on advertising because it works. Once fashion execs learned that people will pay five or six times the appropriate price to wear a brand they saw on TV or a label they heard on the Red carpet, our magazines, airwaves and websites were taken over by ads for luxury fashion products. And young people have been disproportionately targeted.

You should take too much pride in your keen eye for quality apparel and well-designed fashion to blindly imitate what skinny models and Hollywood magazines tell you to wear and how much to spend on it. Even if you like the looks they promote, there are endless options for re-creating upscale styles for a fraction of the retail costs. Especially now.

> *"Fashion companies spend more than $1 billion a year on advertising, trying to keep us from noticing that a hefty segment of that market is also for identical or similar goods at different prices. (For example, a large worldwide manufacturer reports selling jeans with essentially the same manufacturing costs to mass-market chains such as Wal-Mart, mid-market outlets like JC Penney, and high-end designers and department stores,*

> *such as Calvin Klein, at retail prices ranging from about $15 to $65.) Let's not forget that these stores are doing business with the same overseas suppliers, whose products often vary only or mainly by the label. An educated shopper can find bargains this way. But many consumers don't know what they're looking for."*
> —JULIET SCHOR, *The Overspent American* (1999)

Use the following tips to find your inner recessionista and cut your apparel costs by *$1,000* this year.

A TIMELESS TECHNIQUE

The easiest way to save money on clothes is a method I like to call "not buying them." Billions of advertising dollars have turned us into compulsive and irrational consumers—buying new clothes not because we need them but because we get a thrill out of swiping our plastic to acquire our polyester. As American malls have expanded in size during the past 20 years, the practice of social shopping, or shopping for the sake of it, has proliferated*. The average consumer buys 70 pieces of clothing per year, and throws almost as many away within the same period.

3 STRATEGIES FOR SHOPPING MORE EFFICIENTLY

Shop Less. The Simmons survey found that 58 percent of young adults reported going to a shopping mall once every 10 days. By cutting your mall trips in half, you can save more than $900 on clothes that you'd probably end up tossing after two or three wears. Do a fashion fast and spend six weeks without spending a cent on clothing.

ANNUAL SAVINGS: ***$958***

Shop Alone. Young people are the most likely to shop in peer-pressure prone packs. Studies show that people spend more freely and are less likely to buy clearance-rack items or unpopular labels when they shop with friends.

ANNUAL SAVINGS: ***$318***

Shop Comparatively. Simply being an informed consumer rather than an impulse shopper will save you loads.

ANNUAL SAVINGS: ***$277***

---

*This is especially true for younger people. The 2007 Simmons National Consumer Survey found that 20-somethings are least likely to leave a shopping center once they have bought what they needed.

THE DEVIL RUNS PRADA.

If you need any additional motivation to resist that temptation to take a trip to the mall, realize that the fashion industry is home to some of the most socially irresponsible companies on the planet. Clothes designers and retailers knowingly contribute to a number of social ills—a few of them are listed below:

- By increasingly embracing the use of man-made fibers and energy-intensive production cycles, the apparel industry leaves a huge pollution footprint. Each step of the clothing life cycle potentially generates environmental hazards. Polyester, the most widely used manufactured fiber, is made from petroleum while ubiquitous cotton relies on hazardous pesticides. The Environmental Protection Agency has deemed several textile manufacturing facilities to be generators of hazardous waste.
- Retailers profit from the subpar working conditions, child labor and unlivable wages in textile factories in other countries (and in low-income communities in the U.S.). According to figures from the U.S. National Labor Committee, some textile workers in China make as little as 12–18 cents per hour working in hazardous conditions. (Americans purchase approximately 1 billion garments made in China every year.)
- American castoffs are increasingly being shipped to developing countries. Upon arrival, they decimate indigenous businesses and spread Western consumerism to communities where weekly wages are less than the price of a t-shirt. Data from the International Trade Commission indicate that between 1989 and 2003, American exports of used clothing more than tripled, to nearly 7 billion pounds per year.
- If you're a pet lover or animal rights sympathizer, you have 50 million dead fuzzy reasons to stay away from the mall this year. The industry makes some of its largest profits by selling expensive fur products to luxury consumers. According to Infurmation.com, it takes 60 to 100 squirrels to make a fur coat.

SHOPPING ONLINE

The average iLifer spends about $400 a year on online purchases. Shopping online is a great way to save on gas, duck sales taxes and find low-priced items not available at your local mall. Many retailers have made returning online purchases a hassle-free process and more people are opting to buy clothes and shoes without trying them on first. Others try on the clothes in the store and then purchase what they like online at discounted prices. Either way, you should never make a purchase online without first searching for a coupon code. Check out these sites for low-cost apparel and discount codes:

VENDORS

Amazon.com. Not just for textbooks. Amazon has a good selection of cheap clothes from a wide range of designers. Click on the "$0 to $25" link or the "70 percent off or more" category to find the best deals.

Cutesygirl.com. A good site for designer knockoffs at enticing prices. Heels, boots, dresses, bottoms and denim for a fraction of department store prices.

Forever21.com. The physical store tends to be crowded so shop from the comfort of your cubicle. There's a link for men's clothing as well. Items can be returned for store credit at any Forever 21 branch in America. If you want cash back, you'll have to fill out a returns form and ship that frock to their Los Angeles headquarters.

JCP.com. JC Penney consistently produces solid discount codes. Register with the site and receive email alerts when a new coupon code becomes available. **Warning**: Don't give JCP your primary email unless you are okay with hearing about once-a-year blowout sales 2.5 times a week.

6PM.com. A site for low-price shoes that allows you to search by "Biggest Discount" and find some steals.

15dollarstore.com. Jackets, jeans, jewelry, swimwear, sunglasses and more. Everything is $15.

COUPONS

Retailmenot.com. Register with this site to give and get information about the latest sales and discount codes. Users provide the coupon codes and others comment on whether the code worked. Unreliable coupons receive low user-ratings and are demoted to "Under 50 Percent Successful" status on the site.

CouponCabin.com/malls. Before you go to the mall, visit Coupon Cabin and select the name of the shopping center you'll be visiting from an impressive list (organized by city and state). This free site will present a list of every store in your mall of choice that has a printable coupon or online discount code and provide a link so that you can find it.

Pricewatch.com. Pricewatch scans a bunch of retailer sites to find the cheapest apparel on the Web. Shop by price range or by type of item. Search by your preferred brand and find out which online retailer currently has the cheapest Converse Chuck Taylors available.

Google. Before you make an online purchase, search "Coupon + [Store name]" and see if there are any free discount codes floating around in cyberspace.

TOTAL ANNUAL SAVINGS: $625

TWO MORE REASONS TO SHOP ONLINE

Returns. No need worrying about trying to remember where you put that receipt. A digital version is perpetually housed in your email inbox. Log in and fire that baby into the printer.

Tax-Free: *"An additional lure for online shoppers is no sales tax. Currently, in most cases, shoppers are only assessed sales taxes on products purchased from an Internet company that is located in their state, except in states with no sales tax. Although some lawmakers have tried to enact legislation that would make this feature a thing of the past, for the time being it is here to stay and should be used as an additional lure, particularly for customers in areas with high sales tax, such as Illinois at 10 percent."*

—MINTEL INTERNATIONAL, *Budget Shopper*, October 2008

"GREEN" LOOKS GOOD ON YOU: TOWARDS AN ECOLOGICALLY- AND ECONOMICALLY-FRIENDLY WARDROBE

"The average American purchases approximately 70 pounds of fabric per year, with 85 percent ending up in landfills, according to the Institute for Local Self-Reliance. In protest, a new generation of eco-friendly fashion-lovers is finding ways to fight against 'waste couture'—disposable, inexpensive apparel designed to satisfy one's quick fashion needs. Eco-friendly trendsetters are modifying old t-shirts into a tote or refashioning worn-out

> *denim into a miniskirt, and reinterpreting classic, would-be-throwaways into the hottest looks to stay eco-fashionable."*
>
> —SHANI WRIGHT for Fashionincubator.com, *Fabric trashing... or stashing?* August 6, 2008

Not only are these Green fash-tivists staying eco-fly, they're saving a bunch of money by keeping clothes longer, rocking authentic vintage ensembles and buying timeless pieces that outlast fads. Here are a few of their secrets:

Reuse What You Have. Americans buy 70 pounds of clothing per year and forget about scores of neglected treasures in the back of their closets. Do a closet inventory and see if you can put together a few new outfits by marrying previously unrelated items.

ANNUAL SAVINGS: ***$182***

Tweak It. Challenge yourself to recreate one of the season's "must-have" looks using only the items in your wardrobe. Get creative. Bust out a needle and thread or buy some new buttons. Cut up old clothing or sew "supposed-to-be-there" patches over that stubborn stain. Turn that now-hideous dress into a scarf (or a dish rag). Bringing your defunct clothes back to life is a greener alternative to buying a new set of threads every season.

ANNUAL SAVINGS: ***$388***

Buy Vintage at Thrift Shops. There's no longer a stigma associated with used clothing. The National Association of Resale & Thrift Shops reported an average of 35 percent growth in 2008, even as traditional retailers experienced double digit declines. But people aren't shopping at second-hand stores simply because they can't afford anything new. In addition to being socially responsible, stores like Goodwill and the Salvation Army offer great deals on trendy vintage apparel. You can feel good about helping the less fortunate and the planet when you help yourself to that button-down vest for $2. Wash it, then wear it like it's 1929.

> NOTE: These stores tend to have storewide sales so be sure to ask about any upcoming discount days.
>
> NOTE: Check out the "Garage Sale" section of www.craigslist.com.

ANNUAL SAVINGS: ***$341***

Buy Classic. Show a little foresight and buy styles that will stand the test of time. Wise fashion-heads can spot an ephemeral fad with ease and never fill their closets with soon-to-be last season's styles.

Fashion Forward

Seasonal items are often cleared out at phenomenal prices. Stay ahead of the curve by shopping in the off-season. Buying swimsuits in late August and overcoats in early April can lead to savings of 70 percent or more. ***Annual Savings: $295***

Wash Well. The laundering process is the most energy-intensive procedure associated with clothes. By washing only full loads, using the lowest appropriate temperatures when washing, hang drying and avoiding expensive dry-cleaning, you can save money and stay green. *Annual Savings*: ***$43***

Freecycle. If you have clothes that you just can't see yourself wearing ever again, give them away to friends, siblings or second-hand stores instead of throwing them away.

Work It!

If you're a recent grad, you may feel you need to build up your professional wardrobe for the workplace. Before you drive over to Nordstrom or Jos. A. Bank, remember that whatever you spend on work clothes is, in effect, reducing your salary. That is, if you make $40K a year and spend $3,000 on a new wardrobe full of work clothes and shoes, you're really just working for $37,000. Vicki Robin, author of *Your Money or Your Life*, warns that you shouldn't try to convince yourself that the employee clothes you buy are for anything other than work:

> *"Look at those clothes. Would you wear a noose around your neck or walk around on three-inch heels every day if it weren't expected for the Job?"*
>
> —Vicki Robin and Joe Dominguez, *Your Money or Your Life* (2008)

Hair, Makeup and More

HAIR

Let your Lovelocks Down. Wait an extra few weeks before going to the hair salon or the barber (or, even better, embrace DIY hair care). If you get a $20 haircut every three weeks, it'll set you back $346 for the year. If you let your locks grow for an extra two weeks each cycle, you'll save more than ***$150*** (gas included). Cut back on your cuts. Invest in a cap.

ANNUAL SAVINGS: ***$156***

COSMETICS

Buy Beauty Supplies on Sale. Save 80 percent or more on beauty supplies, health-related items and other non-perishables. Wait for your local drugstore to offer a spectacular deal on your favorite beauty product, then stockpile as many as you can.

ANNUAL SAVINGS: $***206***

SAVE OR SPLURGE?

Some beauty essentials are worth the splurge. With other products, you should stick with the drugstore version. Based on independent quality tests, dermatologists' advice and consumer reviews, here's a breakdown of when to save and when to splurge on beauty items.

- **Eyeliner**: Save
- **Eyeshadow**: Splurge
- **Cleansers**: Save
- **Moisturizers**: Save
- **Foundation**: Splurge
- **Concealer**: Splurge
- **Makeup Brushes**: Splave (Splurge or Save)
- **Shampoos and Conditioners**: Save
- **Lipstick* and Lip Gloss**: Save
- **Mascara**: Save
- **Blush and Powders**: Splurge

---

* *"Independent quality tests conducted by Consumer Reports reveal that among a range of brand lipsticks consumers did not find systematic quality differences. Of course, there are different types of lipsticks. But within types, the lipsticks tend to be chemically similar, and users rated none of them better than any other in terms of quality, despite prices ranging from a few dollars to twenty-five dollars."* —JULIET SCHOR, *The Overspent American* (1999)

MANI/PEDI

Do your own nails this year, or have a manicure party with your friends and share nail polish. Follow these tips from *New York* magazine's Cheap Living Guide for inexpensive mani-pedis:

1. Forget expensive hand and foot creams. Body moisturizers or anti-aging lotions are plenty good for hands and feet.
2. Nail files and buffing blocks can be bought in bulk at a beauty supply store like Sally's. Better yet, cut the files in half and the blocks in quarters to make them last longer.
3. The proper way to file is at a 45-degree angle underneath the nail. If your nails are weak, gently file in one direction.
4. Don't overcolor. Wipe polish off one side of the brush, put one dot in the middle of the nail, and fan out until the polish reaches your cuticles.
5. Be patient when drying—15 minutes minimum. To speed up drying time, go for a walk in the cold air. It shrinks the molecules in the lacquer.

ANNUAL SAVINGS: $279

CHAPTER 13

CONCLUSION.

So, that's it. Go forth, have fun and be cheap.

The chapters you've just read cover about 90 percent of the expenditures you will have this year, but there are a bunch of other ways you can save on housing, transportation, food, entertainment and apparel as well as other areas (e.g., insurance). Check out Appendix A for a list of additional resources that will help you save hundreds more this year. Also, visit www.iLifers.com for more personal finance tips, free downloadable budget templates and blogposts by other $15K-Yearers.

Again, $15,000 is just a suggested savings target. If you feel you can save more, go for it. If you can only cut back by $7,000 or $8,000 this year—hey, that's a start.

FINAL WORDS OF ENCOURAGEMENT

As a $15K Year survivor, I owe it to you to let you know that, even with all the tech-heavy tips and strategies that you've read, making it to the finish line will require a lot of good old-fashioned self-control, stamina and resolve. It will be hard at times and, at least once, you'll want to chuck your budget binder out of your 1993 Toyota Tercel and call the whole thing off.

Since you will occasionally question why you're even doing this—why you just turned down a fancy dinner invitation or decided to live with your parents or walked past those gorgeous boots in the store window—I figured it might be helpful to give you a glimpse of what the finish line might look like.

Let's take a before-and-after look at our "standard" iLifer.

OUR STANDARD ILIFER (BEFORE $15K YEAR)

Name: Stan D'ard
Age: 22.5
Occupation: Marketing analyst
Salary: $35,000 (after taxes)
Pre-15K-Year Savings Rate: 3 percent
Pre-$15K-Year Savings: $856
Credit Card Debt: $1,084
Student Loans: $19,007
Average 401(k) contribution: $0 per month

OUR STANDARD ILIFER (AFTER $15K YEAR)

Name: Stan D'ard
Age: 23.5
Occupation: Marketing analyst
Entrepreneurship: Co-founder of **GlobeRock**, a nonprofit that employs seamstresses in Uganda to create accessories for Western luxury buyers (80 percent of the proceeds go towards providing clean drinking water, malaria nets, antiretroviral drugs and educational opportunities in the country's rural communities).
New Salary: $44,000 ($36,500 as a Marketing Analyst, $7,500 as co-founder)
New Savings Rate: 22 percent
New Savings (Emergency Fund): $5,500
Credit Card Debt: $0
Student Loans: $13,307
Average 401(k) contribution: $250 per month (with company match)

Free of credit card debt and strategically investing for the future, he planned to have his student loans paid off in three years and was on track to retire at age 55.

In addition to starting a socially responsible business with his Ugandan-American college roommate, Stan was able to donate $150 with 10 Facebook friends who pooled their money to buy an incubator for a hospital in São Paolo. In his community, he used his marketing skills to help publicize community service events at his church and volunteered once a month with Habitat for Humanity. His soul knew no bounds of joy.

CHANGE THE WORLD.

"Everybody can be great... because everybody can serve."
—MARTIN LUTHER KING, JR.

"Each one should use whatever gift he has received to serve others, faithfully administering God's grace in its various forms."
—1 PETER 4:10

"How wonderful it is that nobody need wait a single moment before starting to improve the world."
—ANNE FRANK

"Change will not come if we wait for some other person or some other time. We are the ones we've been waiting for. We are the change that we seek."
—BARACK OBAMA

"Try not to become a man of success but rather try to become a man of value."
—ALBERT EINSTEIN

"All they asked was that we should continue to remember the poor, the very thing I was eager to do."
—GALATIANS 2:10

"It's time for greatness—not for greed. It's a time for idealism—not ideology. It is a time not just for compassionate words, but compassionate action."
—MARIAN WRIGHT EDELMAN

"It's the little things citizens do. That's what will make the difference. My little thing is planting trees."
—WANGARI MAATHAI

"Every generation needs a new revolution."
—THOMAS JEFFERSON

"Shoot for the moon…"
—Les Brown

Now go out there and make some change.

The world will thank you.

AFTERWORD: The Story Behind the Story

Since *The $15,000 Year* was too time-sensitive to wait for the nine- to 18-month traditional publishing cycle to run its course, I decided to self-publish it. Self-publishing has a much faster turnaround time than traditional publishing and allows the author to assume complete control over the process.

But it also requires the author to assume all the financial costs associated with producing a book—and this usually requires thousands of dollars. As a recent grad without a lot of money, I had to figure out a way to turn this book dream into a reality on a shoestring.

Here's the back-story:

First, embracing the more extreme interpretation of the $15,000 Year, I set out to live on a *maximum* budget of $15,000 for 12 months (or $1,250 per month) while I wrote, published and promoted this book.

I spent six months sharing 200 square-foot dorm rooms with international students, ate more frozen pizzas than I'd like to admit, crashed "Free Food!" functions, put off buying my first car, couch-surfed in L.A. for my vacation and made a bunch of other lifestyle changes that would allow me to quit my part-time job, write full-time and save up enough cash to fund this project.

It was thrilling, frustrating, hilarious, embarrassing, enlightening, disgusting and empowering all at once. But it was most definitely worth it. I'd do it again in a heartbeat.

Second, I realized that, even though I didn't have a lot of cash, I had access to tons of human capital—which, I would find out, usually works just as well as (and sometimes better than) financial capital. I convinced my brother, who received more than his fair share of the family's artistic skills, to design the cover art for the book*. I did a lot of cold-emailing and mass-Facebook-messaging to get my manuscript edited and revised by experts and friends free of charge†. And, since a few of my friends and acquaintances are active bloggers, I got their permission to quote some of their posts.

Finally, what I couldn't accomplish with human capital, I set out to achieve with "techno-capital," or, the cost-cutting power of technology. I hit up the Web for tons of information, advice and testimonials that covered all the steps involved in the book-producing process. After a couple hours, I realized that I could probably handle most of these steps on my own—without spending a dime. After a few more hours of Web surfing, I learned how to set up a publishing company, typeset‡, start a website, create an eBook, work with book printers and copyright my manuscript do-it-yourself style. There were hundreds of blogs, websites, tutorials and free software programs with up-to-date information about how to do all of this, helping me cut expensive middlemen out of the process and save thousands of dollars.

On the marketing side, I discovered it was entirely possible to promote *The $15,000 Year* without hiring a publicist or spending a bunch of money on traditional advertising. Using the power of email, social networking and viral marketing, I was able to publicize this book to the appropriate audiences without breaking budget.

In the end, equipped with little more than a laptop, a few hundred Facebook friends, and a somewhat narcissistic belief that people might actually want to read what I had to say, I was able to publish this book, start a website and found my own publishing company.

But (despite the aforementioned narcissism) I say none of this to toot my own horn.

There are two reasons I think it's important to tell the behind-the-scenes story of this book. First, to let you know that completing the $15,000

---

*Book designers charge up to $2,000.

†Professional editors charge up to $10,000.

‡Typesetting is the process of professionally designing the interior pages of a book using software programs like Adobe InDesign. (Professional designers charge up to $5,000 per book.)

Year is 100-percent doable. It's been done before and many iLifers have already decided to significantly reduce their spending in order to beat the recession. Hopefully, now that you've read the book, you know how to cut back without completely cramping your lifestyle.

Second, to dispel the idea that you have to have loads of money or exclusive industry connections before you can start a business or advance your entrepreneurial idea. To be blunt: This is no longer the case in the digital age. As digital natives, iLifers have the ability to find information and accomplish complex, traditionally costly tasks with an efficiency that no previous generation has ever known. Starting a business (or producing an album, short film or book) has never been easier, less capital-intensive or more exciting and, again, this is the freest time in your life.

Go for it!

Acknowledgements

This book would have not been possible without a ton of support, guidance and inspiration from the following:

First and foremost, a major THANK YOU to my Creator, my Provider, the Rock of my salvation: My Lord and Savior, **Jesus Christ**.

> *"Now to Him who is able to do exceedingly abundantly above all that we ask or think, according to the power that works in us, to Him be glory in the church by Christ Jesus to all generations, forever and ever. Amen."*
>
> —Ephesians 3:20–21

Get to know Him.

To my parents, **Florence and Zacch Olorunnipa**, I could never thank you enough for your love, support, prayers and guidance. I'm blessed to have the very best parents on the planet and this book would have never been possible without you.

To the siblings: **Shola**, major thanks for helping me design the book cover and sharing your thoughts from the very beginning of this project. **Funmi**, thanks for always checking up on me (and for occasionally prodding) and for always giving great life advice. **Yemi**, thanks for the laptop, for laughing at me when I said I had a $100 a month food budget and for letting me sleep on your futon when I was too cheap to rent a place in New York.

I'm extremely grateful to everyone else who contributed to this book in one way or another:

Thank you to **PROF. MICHAEL ROSENFELD** for your course, your comments and your graph. Thanks to **GEOFFREY PAULIN** at the U.S Bureau of Labor Statistics for helping out with the data for this project. **JARED "TERZEL" MURPHY**, many thanks for lending your personal finance critiques. **BRITTANI JACKSON**, thanks a bunch for your "housing" comments. **MS. CAMPS**, your comments on the food section were lovely.

An apologetic shoutout to all my '08 friends whom I neglected during this writing process: **BRITTANI**, **CASSIE**, **DSB**, **JARED**, **JONATHAN**, **KENNETH**, **PORTIA**, **REYNA**, **ROSELYN**, and ___________ (please fill in the blank).

Special thanks to **EKI OSAYANDE**, for keeping me sane during the writing process and sending me weekly texts with free food alerts. *Merci beaucoup!*

AJOKE AGBOOLA, thanks for the words of encouragement and for recruiting me into the Green movement.

To everyone at **STANFORD**: **SASA** folks, **NAIJA** folks, **YOST** folks, **UJ** folks, **ALCF** folks... you all know who you are—*gracias*.

To my Tallahassee family, especially **GO YE CHAPEL**, thanks for your prayers and support.

To my aunts, uncles, cousins and extended family in Nigeria, *E se gan ni...*

To **MR. REGGIE STUART**, much appreciation for taking a chance on a kid from Tallahassee back in 2004 (and for putting up with all the changes over the years).

I owe a special debt of gratitude to **BERNARD AND BONNIE GLASER** and the **GLASER EDUCATIONAL FOUNDATION**, who supported my scholarship and my desire to write a book.

A big thanks to **PAT** and **ROWLAND REBELE** (and **SUSIE**!) for your generosity. My summer-long journalistic quests would not have been possible without you.

To everyone I've left out, apologies and lots of love.

Last but not least, a big Congrats! to the class of 2009 and a shoutout to iLifers all around the world…

Appendix A: Additional Resources

DEALS

- www.dealhack.com
- www.buxr.com
- www.dealnews.com
- www.consumerist.com
- www.consumerreports.com
- www.retailmenot.com
- www.pricewatch.com

FRUGAL LIVING

- www.stretcher.com
- www.ultimatecheapskate.com
- www.freeinnyc.com
- www.livingonadime.com
- www.lacheapskate.blogspot.com
- www.allthingsfrugal.com
- www.frugalliving.about.com
- www.iLifers.com
- www.freecycle.org

PERSONAL FINANCE

- www.jumpstartcoalition.org
- www.20somethingfinance.com

- www.youngandfrugal.com
- www.fool.com
- www.bankrate.com
- www.youngmoneytalks.com
- www.richbythirty.com
- www.mymoney.gov
- www.yacenter.org*

ENTREPRENEURSHIP

- www.brazencareerist.com
- www.mindfrenzy.com
- www.fleethecube.com
- www.youngentrepreneur.com:
- www.theclosetentrepreneur.com
- www.youngandsuccessful.com

*Young Americans Center for Financial Literacy.

APPENDIX B

More on iLifers...

I. iLifers and Civic Engagement

> *"...a generation of student leaders bent on doing good, some graduates of the nation's elite universities are fighting for low-paying teaching jobs the way they once sought jobs on Wall Street."*
>
> —MEGAN GREENWELL for the Washington Post, December 7, 2008

There is considerable evidence (both empirical and anecdotal) that iLifers are concerned about a host of social issues and are actively involved in movements that address the challenges facing the local, national and global communities. Youth interest in public service, volunteering and social entrepreneurship has expanded and intensified during this young century and it shows no signs of slowing down.

Examples illustrating iLifers' civic involvement abound: Teach For America, a program that sends top college graduates to inner-city schools to help educate students, has multiplied in size as the number of applicants jumped from 4,000 in 2000 to more than 35,000 in the 2008–2009 school year. The program, which offered 4,000 slots in 2008, requires a two-year teaching commitment from each participant and reaches nearly half a million underprivileged children annually.

Alternative Spring Break programs, which mobilize college students to spend their spring holidays doing service projects instead of partying, have also become more popular and there are now versions of ASB at more than 200 campuses.

Micro-lending initiatives such as Campus Kiva, which allows college students to connect with and support entrepreneurs in the developing world, have proliferated in recent years.

And, of course, there's the 2008 presidential campaign, in which iLifers' record turnout and unprecedented levels of campaign involvement—overwhelmingly in support of President Barack Obama—effectively tipped the scales of the popular vote in the current president's favor.

THE NEW CIVIC ENGAGEMENT

- Since the mid-1990s, the share of high school seniors who volunteer has nearly tripled.
- Young people donate as much of their income to philanthropic causes as their elders when incomes, education and religious attendance are controlled for. About 70 percent of incoming freshmen in 2007 said it's "essential or very important" to help others in difficulty, the highest that figure has been in 36 years
- In 2008, 23 million Americans in the 18–29 age group years cast a ballot in 2008, up from about 19 million in 2004. A larger share of young people went to the polls in 2008 than in any election since 1972, when the voting age was lowered from 21 to 18.
- *"According to Harvard University's Institute of Politics, almost 60 percent of Millennials are 'personally interested in engaging in some form of public service to help the country.' The ethos of service among Millennials is strongly supported regardless of gender or party affiliation."*

—MORLEY WINOGRAD AND MICHAEL D. HAIS* for NDN, *Reinforcing Obama's Millennial Army*, December 1, 2008

WHY IS THIS HAPPENING?

While it certainly has not been uncommon in modern American history for young people—loaded with spare time, free from familial obligations, and inspired by idealistic goals or anti-authority sentiments—to engage in civic activity and social activism, today's iLifers are distinct in their views, espoused causes, and social movement strategies.

*Winograd and Hais are the authors of *Millennial Makeover: MySpace YouTube, and the Future of American Politics* (2008).

We differ from our generational forebears in a few key areas, including, but definitely not limited to, **diversity, tolerance, global-mindedness** and **tech-based activism**.

DIVERSITY

Census figures and projections show that today's young adults are more racially and ethnically diverse than any other generation in U.S. history. As of 2008, non-whites and Hispanics made up 42 percent of the iLifer population, a more sizeable proportion than the 26 percent among Boomers or the 15 percent among the G.I. gen born between 1901 and 1924. According to federal data, Hispanics represent 15.4 percent of the total U.S. population but 22.4 percent of young adults. African-Americans represent 12.9 percent of the population but 17.3 percent of young adults.

At least one of the ways this increased level of diversity will influence the future is clear. Today's young people will be at the forefront of a cultural transformation in the U.S. in which the country will become more cosmopolitan as the Hispanic, African-American, Asian and Native American populations grow. As the United States progresses towards becoming a minority-majority country by 2050, the generation distinct for its unfamiliarity with racial segregation and its natural comfort with diverse environments will be in the driver's seat.

And it's more than just a numbers thing. The country has been growing more diverse for decades and Boomers and Gen Xers definitely experienced increases in heterogeneity during their formative years as well. But as a result of the lengthened Independent Life Stage, growing college enrollment, and the advent of globe-shrinking digital technology, today's iLifers interact with people of different backgrounds much more frequently than our parents did. Most of us see such our racial, ethnic and socioeconomic interrelations as completely natural.

A 2005 report by the Center for Information and Research on Civic Learning and Engagement, which analyzed a range of social surveys and public opinion polls over time, found that on issues ranging from immigration to race to alternative lifestyles, "the data show that young Americans are the most tolerant age group and are growing more tolerant over time" (2006). In the last 20 years, the share of 18- to 25-year-olds who "completely agree" with the statement "It's alright for blacks and whites to date each other" has shot up from 20 percent to 64 percent.

This increased level of tolerance stems from a number of different sources (aside from the growth in racial diversity). To some extent, it is simply a trend of history. For centuries, younger individuals have tended to be more broad-minded than their fathers. But the high level of openness among today's iLifers is also directly related to the burgeoning importance of the Independent Life Stage. The central thesis of Rosenfeld's *The Age of Independence* is that during this life stage, young adults spend their first years outside of the scrutiny of their parents, giving them an opportunity to develop their own views and opinions. Because young Americans usually spend their period of independence in environments that are more diverse, more tolerant and more pro-tolerance than their parental homes or childhood communities, an increase in open-mindedness is the natural result.

Additionally, even before we left the nest to start our time of independence, many iLifers had been indoctrinated with lessons of acceptance in school and at home. The famous "Middletown" study found that in 1924, mothers believed that the most desirable traits in children were obedience, loyalty to church, and good manners. In 1988, mothers listed independence and tolerance as most desirable.

As a result of these and other factors, iLifers tend to display high levels of appreciation, understanding and interest for lifestyles, opinions and perspectives that differ from our own.

THE FIRST GENERATION OF "GLOBAL CITIZENS"

Raised during a period of rapid globalization, we are the cohort most likely to consider ourselves "global citizens."

iLifers came of age during the tumultuous 1990s, a decade when wars, failed states, infectious diseases and other global humanitarian crises dominated the headlines constantly. Globally, there were three times as many natural disasters in the 1990s as there were in the 1960s with more than 10 times as many victims. There were twice as any armed conflicts. While the average number of refugees per year ranged between 2.5 million and 3.5 million in the 1960s and 1970s, it ballooned to 14.7 million in the 1990s.

Although we certainly aren't the first generation to come of age amid global conflict, the rise of advanced technology and the sheer number of '90s crises made us the first to spend our entire childhoods seeing live, poignant images of those affected by various humanitarian calamities, many of whom were our peers. As we have developed within this "global village" context during the 2000s, we've become quite interested and concerned with what's going on outside our borders. And, to an extent that far exceeds the perspectives of even our postwar parents or Cold War co-workers, we know that our welfare is inextricably intertwined with the wellbeing of our global neighbors.

This isn't just an abstract sentiment of global belonging. It has a major influence on the way we view foreign and domestic policies and sets the tone of our civic engagement. Our political and social views are often at odds with the dominant, mainstream ideologies of our elders in part because we are aware of the alternative perspectives, experiences and life conditions that characterize our peers in other parts of the world.

Our globally-oriented worldview has played a huge role in shaping our countercultural opinions on a number of critical issues. Two that are particularly relevant to this book are climate change and philanthropy. As iLifers—who made up a quarter of the electorate in 2008—grow to make up one third of the voting public by 2016, the way the U.S. conceptualizes these two issues, as well as other global matters, will undoubtedly be completely revamped.

Climate change

iLifers' staunch commitment to the environmental movement is a clear outcome of this global orientation. Most of us realize that the United States has for decades acted as an environmentally inconsiderate global neighbor, consuming a disproportionately large share of the world's resources without doing its fair share to protect the planet from harm. Additionally, members of this cohort understand that it will take a massive multilateral effort and unparalleled levels of international cooperation to address the problem of climate change. According to a 2008 survey by GlobeScan, nearly 90 percent of young adults agree with the statement "world leaders should do 'whatever it takes' to address the issue of climate change."

Philanthropy

We also direct our volunteering and philanthropy more globally than previous generations. More and more young people are giving their time and money to global initiatives through Internet fund-raisers, academic service trips and innovative business schemes like micro-lending programs and "retail philanthropy" (Gap's (PRODUCT) RED™, which supports the fight against AIDS in Africa through apparel sales, is a popular example). The number of applications for the Peace Corps has also risen steadily in recent years.

TECHNO PARTY

Finally, this generation distinguishes itself in its ability to harness the power and convenience of technology to engage in social and political activism. The 2008 campaign season is a perfect case study. Many college students formally took a semester-long leave of absence from school (or, informally took a month or a few weekends off) to help propel the nation's first "wired" president into the White House. Anchored by iLifers such as Facebook co-founder Chris Hughes, President Obama's new media team galvanized millions of young people to get involved in a way that revolutionized the Web as a campaign tool. The campaign benefitted from millions of small donations given via the Web, online phone-banking technology, cell phone directories, text messaging and the organizing capabilities of social networking sites such as Facebook and My.BarackObama.com, which the 24-year-old Hughes designed.

The 2008 elections showcased iLifers' unique ability to spark social movements from dorm rooms with little more than a laptop and cell phone. This serves to highlight the fact that many of our romantic and youthful aspirations to solve major social problems may actually be more realistic than most think, even within our idealistically short timetables.

This combination of idealism, pragmatism and impatience will likely drive social change as the click-and-go generation decides to grab a larger share of political power before its appointed time.

> *"Not since the 1930s have youth had such a large quantitative impact on the national outcome. Rejecting the pundits' outmoded (Generation X) image of the disinterested and disengaged youth voter, these Millennial youth have now made their first major impression on American politics. This is just a prequel. In the coming decades, we predict they will become America's next political powerhouse."*
>
> —NEIL HOWE AND REENA NADLER, *Yes We Can* (2009)

II. iLifers, Intelligence and Information

From IQ scores to grad school enrollment trends, there's a lot of evidence suggesting that iLifers, who came of age during a period of growing academic standards and elevated average levels of educational attainment, represent one of the most cognitively agile cohorts of all time.

- Average SAT scores were higher in 2004 than in 1980, with math scores up 24 points.
- Sixty-four percent of women and 60 percent of men go to college after graduating high school and 85 percent attend full-time.
- In 2008, the number of SAT takers rose to more than 1.5 million , an 8 percent increase from 2003 and a 29.5 percent increase from 1998.
- Of students who began at a 4-year institution in 2003–2004, about one-half had a high school GPA of 3.5 or higher, and about one-fourth had earned credit for courses taken at a college while still in high school.
- Average mathematics scores increased 19 points for eighth graders between 1990 and 2007. Average reading scores were also up, although not as significantly.

- The dropout rates for whites, blacks, and Hispanics have generally showed steady declines since 1976.
- iLifers rank "knowledge" first among every advantage (e.g., money, fame, believing in yourself) that plays a role in achieving success.

III. iLifers and Work

iLifers are beginning to enter the workplace in large numbers and there has been a lot of buzz and speculation about what kind of workers we are, how we interact with our colleagues, and what employers should do to recruit and manage us effectively. Generally, researchers and pundits agree that iLifers approach the workplace—and the idea of employment itself—in ways that differ drastically from previous generations. While some accounts have been pessimistic, most agree that iLifers, possessing a refined dexterity with technology, an affinity for multitasking and high levels of educational attainment, have the *potential* to become the most high-performing workforce in history. But many of our Boomer bosses willingly admit that they are perplexed by our eccentric behavior and not quite sure how to manage us effectively. As more of us enter into full-time employment, it is becoming increasingly clear that many 20th century practices, organizational structures and policies are no longer appropriate for dealing with this new cadre of skilled workers. Here's why:

THE NEW OCCUPATIONAL MOBILITY

iLifers, by definition, are in a transitional phase of life and the extent to which our attitude towards work is shaped by this defining period in our life journeys cannot be overemphasized.

Today's iLifers are nothing like their parents were at the quarterlife marker when it comes to company loyalty or job constancy. Most of us are free of family obligations and will not marry or have children until six or seven years after we enter the workforce. This is our prime opportunity to test out different cities and regions of the country, or maybe travel abroad. It's an opportunity for us to sample career fields and decide what we really want to do in life (college was about finding ourselves and becoming all-around, intelligent individuals). It's a unique time in life when we can give back to society without worrying about the negative effect we might have on our children by taking a low-salary position in the inner city or spending 18 months as an English teacher in Singapore or a medical intern in a South African village.

We see our Independent Life Stage as a distinct time when we are free to take risks, explore the unknown and hopefully have a few interesting stories to tell when all is said and done. And that trumps any feelings of loyalty or allegiance that we're told we're supposed to have for our employers. Many iLifers have parents who exemplified company loyalty for decades only to see their jobs shipped overseas or eliminated in sweeping layoffs at the end of the day. Rather than sitting at the same desk for a decade, today's 20-somethings are choosing to take a little time to explore before settling down into family life.

An extreme but telling example of this experimental approach to work is the story of Daniel Seddiqui, a recent graduate who began a yearlong journey in 2008 that would put him to work in 50 different career fields in 50 different states of the U.S. With a goal of "exploring the diverse careers, environments, and cultures offered in America," the 26-year-old spent a week at each post, working as a rodeo announcer in South Dakota, a medical device manufacturer in Minnesota, a marine biologist in Washington, and experiencing the ins and outs of a bunch of other career fields.

While this type of job fluidity may seem may seem like little more than youthful capriciousness to some, there is in fact method to our mercurial movements. In addition to choosing jobs that will pay our bills and loans, challenge us and allow us to make an impact right away, we want the type of work that will be personally fulfilling. With countless options and a deep-seated belief that we can truly be anything we wish, we realize that sometimes the best way to make a difficult decision is to sample some of the available options. The idea of taking a one-track career path simply because that's the way it's been done for decades does not appeal (or even make sense) to us. We want to have the kind of diverse experiences that will allow us to chart our own unique, even if counterintuitive, paths to the top of our chosen fields. Or, we might just want to take the opportunity to do something random and exciting before beginning the predetermined employment journey through the hierarchy of our preferred industry. Either way, we don't expect any puzzled looks if we say we are considering a career in law, even as we board a plane to Mumbai, where our first full-time employer will be Unite For Sight, a nonprofit organization dedicated to improving eye health and eliminating preventable blindness in impoverished communities.

HIERARCHY, SCHMHIERARCHY...

Accustomed to the quick response of a mouse click, iLifers have a healthy impatience for the type of stagnancy and bureaucratic sluggishness of strict centralized structures. Raised in a digital world that relies on collaboration, we thrive in flat, flexible structures that allow us contribute our skills and maximize efficiency. Generally, we prefer small, self-managing work teams to large, bloated management hierarchies. We favor a fast-paced, dynamic workplace that champions innovation and creativity and see the traditional mantra of "the way we do things around here" as no longer adequate.

Our feelings about workplace stagnancy extend to our attitudes towards upward mobility on the job. If we think we can handle a higher degree of responsibility or play a more central role in shaping the path of the company, one of its divisions or a specific project, we think we should at the very least be given the opportunity to voice our ideas to attentive ears (even if we've only been working for a few months).

TECH-SASSY

We fully expect our workplaces to be wired with all of the digital accoutrements we need to perform at maximum efficiency. At the very least this means high-speed Internet access, a well-designed email system and the smooth integration of Web 2.0 in company transactions.

This is an easy one. We've grown up with this stuff always around and many of us spent our pre-work years at colleges that had the latest software and hardware. We don't expect to regress in this realm when we graduate and enter the workplace. We utilize these tools in order to function at a high rate of productivity and with a low rate of stress. With this in mind, we figure that any company—from art galleries to airliners—that is serious about being competitive and/or efficient in the 21st century should be outfitted with the most appropriate technological equipment for its procedures.

And it's not just about having the latest equipment. We also appreciate a workplace *culture* that fully embraces the problem-solving and time-saving capabilities of digital technology. This means we don't expect or appreciate any strange reactions when we email or IM a coworker whose cubicle is 20 feet away from ours.

Finally, we won't be too happy if our IT department blocks access to Facebook. Actually, we'll be pissed if this happens. Not necessarily because we want to steal time from our boss—which we do—but more fundamentally because we believe that a workplace that shuts itself off from the phenomenon of social networking is one that is clinging to a 20th century mindset and missing out on the potential benefits of Web 2.0 connectivity.

SOCIAL RESPONSIBILITY

Consistent with iLifers' affinity for social activism, we expect our employers to be actively engaged in improving both the local and global communities. An increasingly popular term for this is "social responsibility." This can include everything from maintaining an energy efficient workplace to encouraging community involvement and pro bono work to donating a decent percentage of profits to charity. But it also means not partnering with corporations that knowingly harm the planet or pollute impoverished communities, not engaging in corrupt politics and shady backroom deal-making in D.C., and not indirectly aiding genocide, wars, anarchy or social stagnancy in the developing world through investments, arms sales or other practices.

Most iLifers are not content to simply remain caught up in the day to day hustle and bustle of their departments, unaware of the broader operations of the organization. If our employers are engaged in socially irresponsible behaviors and are profiting by taking advantage of the less fortunate, this is the cohort most likely to know about it, to say something about it, and to expect results.

A 2007 survey by the financial firm Deloitte & Touche found that two-thirds of those 18 to 26 prefer jobs that permit them to contribute to a nonprofit group.

In the age of consumer advocacy sites and customer protest via blog (e.g., www.consumerist.com), corporations have learned quickly that managing the public perception of their brands is crucial to their bottom lines. As more socially conscious iLifers infiltrate the workplace, these companies will be forced to fully embrace, rather than simply advertise, a socially responsible ethos or risk losing highly qualified employees. Many iLifers feel so strongly about social responsibility that they are willing to leave a company if corporate practices aren't in line with their values. Some are simply refusing to apply to the companies that make headlines for CEO extravagance, board member malfeasance or corrupt business practices.

We'd Rather Be Self-Employed

Finally, if our employers fail to take the aforementioned characteristics and expectations into account—if they fail to create workplace environments that provide ample opportunities and rewards; if they cling to outdated business models, promotion practices or technological systems; if they stifle our creativity and input for no other purpose than preserving antiquated hierarchical structures; if they make waste of the planet's resources and neglect her less fortunate—they may lose us to a competitor that is more agreeable, more attentive, more socially-minded and, in our humble opinions, more capable of running a 21st century business than our old bosses. Namely, ourselves.

Dropping out of the corporate workforce to pursue entrepreneurship has become highly attractive option for today's iLifers, half of which list "owning my own business" as a goal. We've come of age hearing stories of young entrepreneurs who dropped out of school or quit their entry-level jobs and went on to found multibillion dollar companies: the Zuckerburgs, the Gateses, the Jobses, and a host of other famed entrepreneurial rock stars that many of us began wishing to emulate after our dreams of being the next Jordan or Spice Girl puttered out during a failed high school tryout or an embarrassing talent show performance. The result: For the first time in history, 18- to 24-year-olds are starting companies at a faster rate than 35- to 44-year-olds, according to a 2007 study by the Global Entrepreneurship Monitor.

The only business environment we've known is one where it is possible to quickly launch a business venture global in scope with minimal upfront costs, low operating expenses, scalability and, most importantly, no permission from traditional gatekeepers. In today's business world, democratizing technology has made it possible for young entrepreneurs, entertainers and e-capitalists to promote their products directly to consumers without appealing to the middlemen who controlled industries such as music and information technology in the past. Innovative ideas and products that may have died in their infancy 35 years ago because a vice president, publisher or A&R didn't find it "groovy" enough, today have the opportunity to reach global audiences without gatekeeper support.

> *"While a kid 30 years ago might have been able to invent a new whirligig, the Internet era has given rise to something new; a cadre of really young kids whose innovations have had global impact. So, even if there aren't more young entrepreneurs than there used to be, they are capable, more than any young generation in the past, of reshaping the global economy. The age of gerontocracy is over."*
>
> —JOHN PALFREY AND URS GASSER, *Born Digital* (2008)

Job-hopper Dan Seddiqui, for example, capitalized on the media buzz surrounding his 50-state employment blitz, started his own website and Youtube channel and began looking at publishing options. To rewind the story a bit, before starting the job tour, Seddiqui had been rejected from more than 40 traditional jobs in the finance sector. Instead of spending 10 or more years climbing the corporate ladder before reaching any level of autonomy, he started his own business with little more than a unique idea, a laptop, a 10-year-old SUV and a road map—and had a ton of fun doing it. He made a little money too.

There are tons of other young people having similar experiences across the country and, even as they don jeans and t-shirts in the office or launch the next hot startup from their dorm rooms, they are pioneering America's future.

Stay tuned for the next iLifer's Guide...

Bibliography

Much of the research for this book was conducted online. For live links to the articles, studies, surveys and reports referenced in this book, visit www.iLifers.com.

> **Note:** Visit www.bls.gov/cex for the most recent data from the Consumer Expenditure Survey.

Here's a list of the physical books that influenced the writing of *The $15,000 Year*:

Almighty God, The. The Bible.

Arnett, Jeffrey Jensen. Emerging Adulthood: The Winding Road from the Late Teens through the Twenties. New York: Oxford UP, USA, 2006.

Balish, Chris. How to Live Well Without Owning a Car: Save Money, Breathe Easier, and Get More Mileage Out of Life. New York: Ten Speed P, 2006.

Clinton, Bill. Giving: How Each of Us Can Change the World. New York: Knopf, 2007.

Dacyczyn, Amy. Complete Tightwad Gazette: Promoting Thrift as a Viable Alternative Lifestyle. New York: Villard Books, 1998.

Frank, Robert H. Luxury Fever: Money and Happiness in an Era of Excess. Princeton, N.J: Princeton UP, 2000.

Frank, Robert. Richistan: A Journey Through the American Wealth Boom and the Lives of the New Rich. New York: Three Rivers P, 2008.

Gandhi, Mohandas. An Autobiography: The Story of My Experiments with Truth. Boston: Beacon P, 1993.

Graaf, John De. Affluenza: The All-Consuming Epidemic. San Francisco, CA: Berrett-Koehler, 2005.

Grader, Rob. The Cheap Bastard's Guide to New York City: A Native New Yorker's Secrets of Living the Good Life. New York: Globe Pequot, 2008.

Grigsby, Mary. Buying Time and Getting By: The Voluntary Simplicity Movement. New York: State University of New York P, 2004.

Gustafson, Kristen. Graduate! Everything You Need to Succeed After College (Capital Ideas) (Capital Ideas). New York: Capital Books, 2002.

How to Survive the Real World: Life After College Graduation Advice from 774 Graduates Who Did (Hundreds of Heads Survival Guides). New York: Hundreds of Heads Books, 2006.

Howe, Neil, and William Strauss. Millennials and the Pop Culture: Strategies For a New Generation of Consumers in Music, Movies, Television, the Internet, and Video Games. LifeCourse Associates, 2006.

Hunt, Mary. The Complete Cheapskate: How to Get Out of Debt, Stay Out, and Break Free From Money Worries Forever. New York: St. Martin's Griffin, 2003.

Josh, Garskof. The Cheap Bastard's Guide to the Good House and Home (Cheap Bastard's). Guilford: Globe Pequot, 2007.

Kansas, Dave. The Wall Street Journal Complete Money and Investing Guidebook. New York: Three Rivers P, 2005.

Kramon, James M. What They Don't Teach You in College: A Graduate's Guide to Life on Your Own. Grand Rapids: Sphinx, 2006.

Laermer, Richard and Mark Simmons. Punk Marketing: Get off Your Ass and Join the Revolution. New York: Collins Business, 2007.

Malhotra, Monte. The Young Investor's Guide to Retiring Young. Baltimore: PublishAmerica, 2007.

Orman, Suze. The Money Book for the Young, Fabulous and Broke. New York: Riverhead Hardcover, 2005.

Palfrey, John, and Urs Gasser. Born Digital: Understanding the First Generation of Digital Natives. New York: Basic Books, 2008.

Robin, Vicki and Joe Dominguez. Your Money or Your Life: 9 Steps for Transforming Your Relationship with Money and Achieving Financial Independence. New York: Penguin (Non Classics), 2008.

Rosenfeld, Michael J. The Age of Independence: Interracial Unions, Same-Sex Unions, and the Changing American Family. New York: Harvard UP, 2007.

Schor, Juliet B. The Overworked American: The Unexpected Decline of Leisure. New York: Basic Books, 1993.

—The Overspent American: Why We Want What We Don't Need. New York: Harper Paperbacks, 1999.

Segal, Jerome M. Graceful Simplicity: Toward a Philosophy and Politics of Simple Living. New York: H. Holt & Co., 1999.

Wharton, Robert M. Book Industry Trends 2007. New York: Book Industry Study Group, 2007.

Yeager, Jeff. The Ultimate Cheapskate's Road Map to True Riches: A Practical (and Fun) Guide to Enjoying Life More by Spending Less. New York: Broadway, 2007.